Church of Scotland, Church Service Society

Euchologion

A book of common order - being forms of worship. Second Edition

Church of Scotland, Church Service Society

Euchologion

A book of common order - being forms of worship. Second Edition

ISBN/EAN: 9783337291518

Printed in Europe, USA, Canada, Australia, Japan

Cover: Foto ©Lupo / pixelio.de

More available books at **www.hansebooks.com**

EUCHOLOGION

OR

A BOOK OF COMMON ORDER

BEING

FORMS OF WORSHIP

ISSUED BY

The Church Service Society

"Juxta laudabilem Ecclesiæ Scotiæ Reformatæ formam et ritum."
—ARCHBISHOP GRINDAL, 1582.

SECOND EDITION, REVISED AND ENLARGED

WILLIAM BLACKWOOD AND SONS
EDINBURGH AND LONDON
MDCCCLXIX

Contents.

	PAGE
PREFACE,	vii
TABLE OF PSALMS AND LESSONS OF HOLY SCRIPTURE FOR EACH LORD'S DAY IN THE YEAR, ETC.,	1

MATERIALS FOR THE CONSTRUCTION OF A SERVICE FOR PUBLIC WORSHIP ON THE LORD'S DAY—

	PAGE
SENTENCES OF SCRIPTURE,	12
I. INTRODUCTORY COLLECTS,	21
II. CONFESSIONS,	28
III. PRAYERS FOR PARDON AND PEACE,	39
IV. SUPPLICATIONS,	44
V. PRAYERS,	57
VI. THANKSGIVINGS,	63
VII. PRAYERS FOR ILLUMINATION,	74
VIII. ASCRIPTIONS OF PRAISE,	80
IX. PRAYERS AFTER SERMON,	83
X. INTERCESSIONS,	88
XI. CONCLUDING COLLECTS,	114
XII. GENERAL COLLECTS,	118

XIII. CANTICLES,	148
XIV. BENEDICTIONS,	149
XV. MORNING AND EVENING SERVICES,	151
SACRAMENT OF BAPTISM,	185
ADMISSION OF YOUNG PERSONS TO THE LORD'S SUPPER,	198
THE SACRAMENT OF THE LORD'S SUPPER,	215
THE SOLEMNIZATION OF MATRIMONY,	241
MANUAL FOR THE BURIAL OF THE DEAD,	254
I. SERVICE AT THE HOUSE,	260
II. SERVICE IN PUBLIC,	275
ORDINATION SERVICE,	294

Preface.

IN complying with the demand for a second edition of 'Euchologion,' the Editors are able to offer a collection of Prayers and Services which is more extensive than the last, and they hope in many respects an improvement upon it. Whatever explanation of the nature and objects of the Society which they represent may still be needed, will be found in the extract here given from the preface to the first edition.

"The Church Service Society is an Association of Ministers of the Church of Scotland. The formation of a Clerical Society or Club, which should occupy itself with the improvement of the Services of the Church, had for some time been talked of and much desired by many of the clergy, when early in January

1865 a few ministers met in Glasgow to consider the matter. The result of their conference was, that a meeting of ministers was held in Glasgow on the 31st January of that year, at which the Society was formally constituted; and a constitution adopted, of which the following rules are a part:—

"'That the name of the Society shall be The Church Service Society.

"'That none but ordained ministers of the Church of Scotland shall be eligible as members.

"'That the object of the Society shall be the study of the liturgies, ancient and modern, of the Christian Church, with a view to the preparation and ultimate publication of certain forms of prayer for public worship, and services for the administration of the sacraments, the celebration of marriage, the burial of the dead, &c.'

"At the same meeting a committee was appointed, and named the Editorial Committee, to which it was remitted 'to consider what steps it is advisable to take in order to carry out the intention of the Society.' By this Committee a Report was laid before the Society on the 31st March 1865, from which the following passages, which indicate with sufficient clearness the Society's views, are extracted :—' Whether the introduction of a liturgy is desirable and possible, or undesirable and impossible, the Society does not propose to discuss. Upon that question there may be, within it, diversity of opinion; but on this point there can be none —That the introduction of a liturgy into any Church whose worship has not been hitherto liturgical, must be a measure long considered, slowly matured, and ultimately carried, not by any private association of clergymen, but by the public, official, and constitutional action of the Church herself.' The justice of these words will be generally admitted; and at the same time it will be conceded, that between the bondage of a positive liturgy and the poverty of an absolutely extemporaneous service, bound by no rule—free to vary, not only in substance but in form, from week to week—simple to bareness, and yet with little order or uniformity in its simplicity—there is a wide chasm, which it is a most legitimate and pious design to attempt to fill up with the best material that one can find.

"There appear to be, at present, two somewhat powerful currents of feeling in the Church, which are generally supposed to run counter to each other, but which in reality do not, or at least need not do so. The one feeling is that of sincere attachment to the simplicity of our customary worship; the other is an earnest desire for a worship more solemn, uniform, and devout than (in tone and aspect at least) our service generally is. To a large number of estimable people that simple service is dear. With it, rightly or wrongly, is bound up much of their spiritual life; round it gather most of their religious associations. To an equal number, probably, that simplicity is not attractive, because it is not, in their experience, the parent or associate of like good influences. But what has rendered the service of our sanctuaries heavy and profitless to them is not its simplicity, but what is too often combined therewith, and may be as readily associated with the simplest as with the most elaborate service—its lifelessness, its lack of devotion in spirit and in form. It has appeared to the Committee that the true remedy for this defect, and the true reconciliation of these two feelings, are to be found in the filling up of the simple forms which are valued by the one, with the earnest devotions which are desired by the other ; by doing, in short, what the Society proposes to attempt, preparing or collecting forms of prayer as full and as suggestive of solemn, earnest, fervent devotion as words can be, and binding these into the simple order of our existing worship.

" It is very possible that in some minor points of arrangement that order may be improved (and ample freedom for such improvement is guaranteed by our Directory); but, on the whole, our plain service is suited to the constitution of our Church and to the genius of our people, and may not be radically departed from."

We have only to add that, generally, references to the source of the prayers are appended. The reference is not necessarily to the original source, but sometimes to that, and sometimes only to the book or liturgy in which the prayer is commonly found.

Table

of

Lessons for Public Worship.

WHILE the public reading of Holy Scripture is enjoined by precept and example in Scripture itself, and is declared by the Reformed Church, in all its branches, to be a part of the worship of God, essential both as an act of homage to Him and a means of edifying the Church, experience has proved that the full and regular reading of Scripture in divine service is permanently secured only by the use of a Table of Lessons—that is, Readings—in the hands of minister and people.

The Assembly of Divines at Westminster, while, as is well known, most desirous to promote the exposition and preaching of the Word, entertained at the same time a very deep conviction of the importance of public readings of Scripture uninterrupted by any comment; and, objecting to the usage which had prevailed in the English and other Reformed Churches, of reading on the Lord's day only such selected portions as were set forth in the respective Tables of Lessons, and of Gospels and Epistles, declared it to be "*requisite that all the canonical books should be read over in order, that the people may be better acquainted with the whole body of the Scriptures;*" adding that, "*ordinarily, where the reading in either Testament endeth on one Lord's day, it is to begin the next.*" In thus seeking to give greater fulness and prominence to the public reading of Scripture, and specially commending "the frequent reading" of the Psalms,* they state it to be "*convenient that ordinarily one chapter of each Testament be read at every meeting, and*" (not supposing that *less* would be read) "*sometimes more, where the chapters be short, or the coherence of matter requireth it.*" But no precise scheme having been set forth by which these general rules might be

---

* "To read a portion of the Psalms before the chapters."
—Gillespie's Notes on the Westminster Assembly.

carried into effect, and the practice thereby recommended, secured, and strengthened by a new uniformity of usage throughout the Church, the result, as is well known, was that, in the Churches which adopted the Westminster standards, the public reading of Scripture, instead of becoming more regular and copious than under the discarded tables, became, through the want of such support as theirs, more irregular and scanty; until at length God's plain, powerful, and blessed Word ceased to have any place in God's service, which (except the singing of short portions of the Psalms in the metrical version) came to consist entirely of prayers and preaching, such as the ability and inclination of individual ministers might supply.

The evils of an omission so disrespectful to the divine Word, so inconsistent with the character of a Reformed Church, and so detrimental to the service of the sanctuary and the wholesome instruction of the people, are now generally admitted; and, within recent years, the reading of a portion of each Testament at each meeting for public worship has been in many places resumed. But with the returning sense of the importance of this part of public worship, there is a growing feeling of the necessity for a Table of Lessons, as at once a guide, a bond of joint action, and a source of strength, to those who have its revival at heart.

The following biennial table, while securing the advantages of a calendar, obviates in a considerable degree, and probably as far as will be found possible, the objection made, not without reason, to the tables in use in most Churches, that they present only a small portion—varying little or nothing from year to year—of the whole Scripture for public reading. It is comprehensive as well as simple, including the whole of the Gospels and the greater part of the other books of the New Testament. A few of the most instructive and impressive chapters of the Old Testament are omitted from the general table, and reserved for special services, as indicated in a short supplementary table. In regard to those special services which are *commemorative*, the propriety and benefit of such services appear to be generally recognised, apart from the question of set times. It may, however, be observed that a continued refusal to concur with the great body of Christians throughout the world in such stated annual acts of commemoration, seems somewhat unreasonable on the part of those who observe centenary and other solemnities in commemoration of events worthy indeed of religious remembrance, but not, without irreverence, to be compared to the great events in the redemption of the world. In the Table of First Lessons for Evening Service, the books of the Prophets have been arranged in the most generally received chronological order, with a view to their being better understood by the unlearned than when read or heard in the usual order; and for the sake of variety, the Book of Proverbs, in its distinct divisions, which are unconnected with each other, and the Book of Ecclesiastes, have been inserted at various places among prophetical writings. In Churches where there is only one service on the Lord's day, the Table of Lessons will serve for four years.

Table of Psalms and Lessons of Holy Scripture for each Lord's Day in the Year, &c.

TABLE OF PSALMS AND LESSONS OF HOLY SCRIPTURE FOR EACH LORD'S DAY IN THE YEAR.

First Year.*

Lord's Day of the Year.	Month and Day.	MORNING SERVICE.			EVENING SERVICE.		
		1 Lesson.	Psalms.	2 Lesson.	1 Lesson.	Psalms.	2 Lesson.
1	Jan. 1, 2, 3, 4, 5, 6, 7	Genesis 1	1, 2	Matt. 1, v. 18; & 2	Proverbs 1	3, 4	Acts 1
2	Jan. 8, 14	2	5, 6	3	2	7, 8	2, to v. 22
3	15, 21	3	9	4	3	10, 11	2, v. 22
4	22, 28	4	12, 13, 14, 15	5, to v. 21	4	16, 17	3
5	Feb. 29, Feb. 4	5	18	5, v. 21	5	19	4
6	Feb. 5, 11	6	20, 21	6	6	22	5
7	12, 18	7	23, 24	7	7	25, 26	6
8	19, 25	8	27, 28	8	8	29, 30	8
9	Mar. 26, Mar. 3	9 to v. 20	31	9	Jonah 1, 2	32	9, to v. 23
10	Mar. 4, 10	11, to v. 10; & 12, to v. 10	33	10	Joel 3, v. 9	34	9, v. 23
11	11, 17	13	35	11	Amos 9	36	10
12	18, 24	15	37	12, to v. 22	Micah 4	38	11
13	25, 31	21	39, 40	12, v. 22	6	41	12
14	Apr. 1, 7	28	42, 43	13, to v. 31	Hosea 6	44	16
15	Apr. 8, 14	37	45	13, v. 31	13	46, 47	17
16	15, 21	41, v. 14	48	14	Nahum 1	49	20, v. 17
17	22, 28	42	50	15	Proverbs 10	51	26
18	29, May 5	43	52, 53, 54	16	11	55	27
19	May 6, 12	44	56, 57	17	12	58, 59	28
20	13, 19	46, to v. 8; & 47, to v. 13	60, 61	18	13	62, 63	Romans 1, to v. 25
21	20, 26	48	64, 65	19	14	66, 67	2
22	27, June 2	49	68	20	15	69	3
23	June 3, 9	50	70, 71	21, to v. 23	16	72	4
24	10, 16	Exodus 2	73	21, v. 23	17	74	5
25	17, 23	3	75, 76	22	18	77	6
26	24, 30	4	78	23	19	79	7
27	July 1, 7	5	80, 81	24	20	82, 83	8
28	8, 14	7	84, 85	25	21	86	12

PSALMS AND LESSONS OF SCRIPTURE.

			1 Lesson.	Psalms	2 Lesson.
29	July 15	July 21	10	87, 88	26, to v. 36
30	— 22	— 28	— 15	90, 91	26, v. 36
31	Aug. 5	Aug. 4	16, to v. 20	94, 95	27, to v. 32
32	— 12	— 11	— 17	97, 98	27, v. 32
33	— 19	— 18	— 32	100, 101	— 28
34	— 26	— 25	— 34	103	Mark 1
35	Sept. 2	Sept. 1	— 40, v. 17	105	— 2
36	— 9	— 8	Levit. 25, to v. 24	107	— 3
37	— 16	— 15	— 26	109, 110	— 4
38	— 23	— 22	Numbers 11	114, 115	— 5
39	— 30	— 29	13, v. 17	118	6, to v. 30
40	Oct. 7	Oct. 6	— 14	119, v. 17 to 41	6, v. 30
41	— 14	— 13	— 16	119, v. 57 to 81	— 7
42	— 21	— 20	— 20, & 21, to v. 10	119, v. 97 to 121	— 8
43	— 28	— 27	— 22	119, v. 137 to 161	9, to v. 30
44	Nov. 4	Nov. 3	— 23	120, 121, 122	9, v. 30
45	— 11	— 10	— 24	123, 127, 128	10, to v. 32
46	— 18	— 17	Deut. 1, v. 19	132, 133	10, v. 32
47	— 25	— 24	— 4, to v. 41	136	— 11
48	Dec. 2	Dec. 1	— 6	139	— 12
49	— 9	— 8	— 9	142, 143	— 13
50	— 16	— 15	— 10	145	14, to v. 32
51	— 23	— 22	— 30	147	14, v. 32
52	— 30	— 29	— 33	149	— 15
53	—	— 31	— 34	103	— 16

29			13
30			14
31			15, to v. 13
32			1 Cor. 1, to v. 25
33			— 2
34			— 3
35			— 9
36			— 10
37			— 12
38			— 13
39			15, to v. 20
40			15, v. 20
41			2 Cor. 4
42			— 5
43			— 6
44			— 12
45			Galat. 3
46			— 5
47			— 6
48			Ephes. 1
49			— 2
50			— 3
51			— 4
52			— 5
53			— 6

Commemoration of	1 Lesson.	Psalms.	2 Lesson.	1 Lesson.	Psalms.	2 Lesson.
Christ's Nativity	Isaiah 9, v. 2 to v. 9	85	Luke 2 to v. 15	Isaiah 7, v. 10 to v. 17	132	John 1 to v. 19; or Heb. 1
Crucifixion	Genesis 22, to v. 20; or Leviticus 16	22, 40	John 18 or 19	Isaiah 53; or Zech. 13	88, 143	Philip. 2: or Heb. to v. 26
Resurrection	Exodus 12, or 14	2, 45	John 20; or Matt. 28	Isaiah 52, or 60	98, 118	Acts 2, v. 22; or Romans 6
Ascension	2 Kings 2, to v. 19	24, 47	Luke 24, v. 44	—	—	—
The descent of the Holy Ghost	Isaiah 49, or 61	68 or 72	John 14, v. 15; or Acts 4	—	—	—
Humiliation for Sins under Calamity	Isaiah 59	51, 130	Luke 6, v. 20	Isaiah 11, or 35	110, 67	Acts 2, or 19, to v. 21
Thanksgiving for Harvest	Daniel 9	25	Hebrews 12	Hosea 14	6, 32	2 Peter 3
other Mercies	Deut. 8, or 11	65, 147	Romans 13	Jonah 3	102	1 Peter 4
	Isaiah 12	103, 116, or 145	Philip. 4			

* Note.—The Table for the First Year is to be used in those years of which the number is odd, as 1867-69-71, &c.; the Table for the Second Year in those of which the number is even, as 1868-70-72, &c.

TABLE OF PSALMS AND LESSONS OF HOLY SCRIPTURE FOR EACH LORD'S DAY IN THE YEAR.

Second Year.*

Lord's Day of the Year.	Month and Day.	MORNING SERVICE. 1 Lesson.	Psalms.	2 Lesson.	EVENING SERVICE. 1 Lesson.	Psalms.	2 Lesson.
1	Jan. 1, 2, 3, 4, 5, 6, 7	Joshua 3	1, 2	Luke 1, to v. 39	Isaiah 54	3, 4	Philip. 1
2	— 8 Jan. 14	— 5	5, 6	— 1, v. 39	— 55	7, 8	— 2
3	— 15 — 21	— 7	9	— 2	— 56	10, 11	— 3
4	— 22 — 28	— 24	12, 13, 14, 15	— 3, to v. 23	— 57	16, 17	— 4
5	— 29 Feb. 4	Judges 2	18	— 4	— 58	19	Col. 1
6	Feb. 5 — 11	— 6	20, 21	— 5	— 62	22	— 2
7	— 12 — 18	— 7	23, 24	— 6	— 63	25, 26	3 & 4, to v. 7
8	— 19 — 25	Ruth 1	27, 28	— 7	— 64	29, 30	1 Thess. 4
9	— 26 Mar. 3	1 Samuel 3	31	— 8, to v. 26	— 65		— 5
10	Mar. 4 — 10	— 4	33	— 8, v. 26	— 66	32	2 Thess. 2
11	— 11 — 17	— 12	35	— 9, to v. 28		34	— 3
12	— 18 — 24	— 15	37	— 9, v. 28	Zeph. 3, v. 8	36	1 Tim. 4
13	— 25 — 31	— 16	39, 40	— 10	Hab. 2	38	— 6
14	April 1 — 7	17, v. 32	42, 43	— 11, to v. 29	3	41	2 Tim. 3
15	— 8 — 14	— 24	45	— 11, v. 29	Jeremiah 8	44	Titus 2
16	— 15 — 21	2 Samuel 7	48	— 12, v. 35	— 9	46, 47	Philemon
17	— 22 — 28	12, to v. 24	50	— 12, v. 35	— 17, to v. 19	49	Hebrews 1
18	— 29 May 5	— 15	52, 53, 54	— 13	— 18, to v. 18	51	— 2
19	May 6 — 12	— 17	56, 57	— 14	— 31, to v. 21	55	— 3
20	— 13 — 19	— 18	60, 61	— 15	— 31, v. 21	58, 59	— 4
21	— 20 — 26	19, to v. 23	64, 65	— 16	— 33	62, 63	— 5
22	— 27 June 2	19, v. 23	68	— 17	Lam. 3, v. 22 to v. 60	66, 67	— 6
23	June 3 — 9	1 Kings 3	70, 71	— 18	Obadiah	68	— 9
24	— 10 — 16	— 4	73	— 19	Ezekiel 1	72	— 10
25	— 17 — 23	— 5	75, 76	— 20	— 8	74	— 11
26	— 24 — 30	— 6	78	— 21	— 27	77	— 12
27	July 1 — 7	8, to v. 22	80, 81	— 22, to v. 39	— 28, to v. 20	79	— 13
28	— 8 — 14	8, v. 22	84, 85	— 22, v. 39	— 33, to v. 21	82, 83	James 1
					— 34, v. 11	86	— 2

PSALMS AND LESSONS OF SCRIPTURE.

SELECTED PSALMS.

MONTHLY COURSE.

Day of Month	Morning.	Evening.
1	1, 2, 3	4, 5
2	8, 9	15, 16
3	17, 19	23, 24
4	25, 26	27, 28
5	29, 30	31, 32
6	33, 34	36
7	37, 38	39, 40
8	42, 43	45
9	46, 47	49
10	50	51, 53
11	55	57
12	61, 62, 63	65
13	66, 67	68
14	71	72
15	73	77
16	84, 85	86
17	89, 90	91, 92
18	93, 94, 95	96, 97, 98
19	99, 100, 101	102
20	103	104
21	107	110, 111, 112
22	113, 115	116, 117
23	118	119, 1-32
24	119, 33-72	119, 73-104
25	119, 105-144	119, 145-176
26	121, 122, 123	125, 126, 127, 128
27	130, 131, 132	133, 134, 135
28	136, 138	139
29	142, 143	144
30	145, 146	147
31	148, 149	150

Where more Psalms than one are indicated for any Service, one or more of them may be used at discretion.

* NOTE.—The Table for the First Year is to be used in those years of which the number is odd, as 1867-69-71, &c.: the Table for the Second Year in those of which the number is even, as 1868-70-72, &c.

Materials for the Construction of a Service for Public Worship on the Lord's Day.

Sentences of Scripture,

Of which one or more may be read or recited as introductory to the service of God.

OFFER the sacrifices of righteousness, and put your trust in the Lord.—Psalm iv. 5.

Behold, the eye of the Lord is upon them that fear Him, upon them that hope in His mercy.—Psalm xxxiii. 18.

The eyes of the Lord are upon the righteous, and His ears are open unto their cry.—Psalm xxxiv. 15.

The Lord is nigh unto them that are of a broken heart; and saveth such as be of a contrite spirit.—Psalm xxxiv. 18.

Though the Lord be high, yet hath He respect unto the lowly; but the proud He knoweth afar off.—Psalm cxxxviii. 6.

The Lord is nigh unto all them that call upon Him, to all that call upon Him in truth. He will fulfil the desire of them that fear Him ; He also will hear their cry, and will save them.—Psalm cxlv. 18, 19.

He that covereth his sins shall not prosper; but whoso confesseth and forsaketh them shall have mercy.—Prov. xxviii. 13.

Look unto me, and be ye saved, all the ends of the earth ; for I am God, and there is none else.—Isa. xlv. 22.

Seek ye the Lord while He may be found, call ye upon Him while He is near; let the wicked forsake his way, and the unrighteous man his thoughts ; and let him return unto the Lord, and He will have mercy upon him ; and to our God, for He will abundantly pardon.—Isa. lv. 6, 7.

Thus saith the high and lofty One that inhabiteth eternity, whose name is Holy ; I dwell in the high and holy place, with him also that is of a contrite and humble spirit, to revive the spirit of the humble, and to revive the heart of the contrite ones. For I will not contend for ever, neither will I be always wroth; for the spirit should fail before me, and the souls which I have made.—Isa. lvii. 15, 16.

Thus saith the Lord, the heaven is my throne, and the earth is my footstool ; where is the house that ye build unto me ? and where is the place of my rest? For all those things hath mine hand made, and all those things are mine,* saith the Lord; but to this man will I look, even to him that is poor, and of a contrite spirit, and trembleth at my word.—Isa. lxvi. 1, 2.

As I live, saith the Lord God, I have no pleasure in the death of the wicked; but that the wicked turn from his way and live: turn ye, turn ye from your evil ways; for why will ye die, O house of Israel?—Ezek. xxxiii. 11.

Take with you words, and turn to the Lord: say unto Him, Take away all iniquity, and receive us graciously; so will we render the calves of our lips—the sacrifice of praise.—Hosea xiv. 2; Heb. xiii. 15.

Rend your heart, and not your garments, and turn unto the Lord your God; for He is gracious and merciful, slow to anger, and of great kindness, and repenteth him of the evil.—Joel ii. 13.

From the rising of the sun even unto the going down of the same, my name shall be great among the Gentiles; and in every place incense shall be offered unto my name, and a pure offering; for my name shall be great among the heathen, saith the Lord of Hosts.—Mal. i. 11.

Repent ye; for the kingdom of heaven is at hand.—Matt. iii. 2.

Ask, and it shall be given you; seek, and ye

* Marginal reading.

shall find ; knock, and it shall be opened unto you ; for every one that asketh receiveth ; and he that seeketh findeth ; and to him that knocketh, it shall be opened.—Matt. vii. 7, 8.

Where two or three are gathered together in my name, there am I in the midst of them.—Matt. xviii. 20.

The hour cometh, and now is, when the true worshippers shall worship the Father in spirit and in truth ; for the Father seeketh such to worship Him. God is a Spirit ; and they that worship Him must worship Him in spirit and in truth.—John iv. 23, 24.

God resisteth the proud, and giveth grace to the humble. Humble yourselves therefore under the mighty hand of God, that He may exalt you in due time ; casting all your care upon Him, for He careth for you.—1 Pet. v. 5-7.

Draw nigh to God, and He will draw nigh to you.—James iv. 8.

There be many that say, Who will show us any good ? Lord lift Thou up the light of Thy countenance upon us.—Psalm iv. 6.

Give ear to my words, O Lord, consider my meditation. Hearken unto the voice of my cry, my King, and my God ; for unto Thee will I pray.—Psalm v. 1, 2.

I will come into Thy house in the multitude of Thy mercy; and in Thy fear will I worship toward Thy holy temple.—Psalm v. 7.

Let the words of my mouth, and the meditation of my heart, be acceptable in Thy sight, O Lord, my strength and my Redeemer.—Psalm xix. 14.

I will wash my hands in innocency; so will I compass Thine altar, O Lord; that I may publish with the voice of thanksgiving, and tell of all Thy wondrous works. Lord, I have loved the habitation of Thy house, and the place where Thine honour dwelleth.—Psalm xxvi. 6-8.

One thing have I desired of the Lord, that will I seek after; that I may dwell in the house of the Lord all the days of my life, to behold the beauty of the Lord, and to inquire in His temple. —Psalm xxvii. 4.

How excellent is Thy loving-kindness, O God! Therefore the children of men put their trust in the shadow of Thy wings. They shall be abundantly satisfied with the fatness of Thy house; and Thou shalt make them drink of the river of Thy pleasures. For with Thee is the fountain of life; in Thy light shall we see light.—Psalm xxxvi. 7-9.

O Lord, rebuke me not in Thine anger; neither chasten me in Thy hot displeasure. For I will declare mine iniquity; I will be sorry for my sin.—Psalm xxxviii. 1, 18.

Lord be merciful unto me: heal my soul; for I have sinned against Thee.—Psalm xli. 4.

Why art thou cast down, O my soul? and why art thou disquieted within me? Hope thou in God, for I shall yet praise Him, who is the health of my countenance and my God.—Psalm xlii. 11.

O send out Thy light and Thy truth: let them lead me; let them bring me unto Thy holy hill, and to Thy tabernacles. Then will I go unto the altar of God, unto God my exceeding joy: yea, upon the harp will I praise Thee, O God, my God.—Psalm xliii. 3, 4.

I acknowledge my transgressions; and my sin is ever before me.—Psalm li. 3.

Hide Thy face from my sins, and blot out all mine iniquities. Create in me a clean heart, O God; and renew a right spirit within me. Cast me not away from Thy presence; and take not Thy Holy Spirit from me.—Psalm li. 9-11.

The sacrifices of God are a broken spirit; a broken and a contrite heart, O God, Thou wilt not despise.—Psalm li. 17.

My soul, wait thou only upon God; for my expectation is from Him.—Psalm lxii. 5.

Blessed is the man whom Thou choosest, and causest to approach unto Thee, that he may dwell in Thy courts: we shall be satisfied with the goodness of Thy house, even of Thy holy temple.—Psalm lxv. 4.

How amiable are Thy tabernacles, O Lord of Hosts! My soul longeth, yea, even fainteth for the courts of the Lord: my heart and my flesh crieth out for the living God.—Psalm lxxxiv. 1, 2.

A day in Thy courts is better than a thousand; I had rather be a doorkeeper in the house of my God, than to dwell in the tents of wickedness.—Psalm lxxxiv. 10.

Open to me the gates of righteousness. I will go into them, and I will praise the Lord.—Psalm cxviii. 19.

Our help is in the name of the Lord, who made heaven and earth.—Psalm cxxiv. 8.

Out of the depths have I cried unto Thee, O Lord. Lord, hear my voice; let Thine ears be attentive to the voice of my supplications. If Thou, Lord, shouldest mark iniquities, O Lord who shall stand? But there is forgiveness with Thee, that Thou mayest be feared.—Psalm cxxx. 1-4.

Let Israel hope in the Lord; for with the Lord there is mercy, and with Him is plenteous redemption. And He shall redeem Israel from all his iniquities.—Psalm cxxx. 7, 8.

Enter not into judgment with Thy servant; for in Thy sight shall no man living be justified. —Psalm cxliii. 2.

I stretch forth my hands unto Thee; my soul thirsteth after Thee, as a thirsty land. Hear me speedily, O Lord: my spirit faileth: hide not Thy face from me.—Psalm cxliii. 6, 7.

Cause me to hear Thy loving-kindness in the morning; for in Thee do I trust: cause me to know the way wherein I should walk; for I lift up my soul unto Thee.—Psalm cxliii. 8.

Deliver me, O Lord, from mine enemies; I flee unto Thee to hide me. Teach me to do Thy will; for Thou art my God: Thy Spirit is good; lead me into the land of uprightness.—Psalm cxliii. 9, 10.

Let us search and try our ways, and turn again to the Lord; let us lift up our hearts with our hands to God in the heavens. We have transgressed and have rebelled.—Lam. iii. 40-42.

To the Lord our God belong mercies and forgivenesses, though we have rebelled against Him; neither have we obeyed the voice of the Lord our God, to walk in His laws which He set before us.—Dan. ix. 9, 10.

I will arise and go to my father, and will say unto him, Father, I have sinned against Heaven, and before thee, and am no more worthy to be called thy son.—Luke xv. 18, 19.

If we say that we have no sin, we deceive ourselves, and the truth is not in us. If we confess our sins, He is faithful and just to forgive us our sins, and to cleanse us from all unrighteousness. —1 John i. 8, 9.

PRAYERS.

The Society recommend that, in the use of these prayers, the following order should be observed :—

First Prayer.

Introductory Collect.
Confession of Sin.
Prayer for Pardon and Peace.
Supplications.
Concluding Collect.

Second Prayer.

Thanksgiving.
Prayer for Illumination (before Sermon).

Third Prayer.

Collect (after Sermon).
General Intercession.
Concluding Prayer.

The Lord's Prayer may conclude either the First or Second Prayer.

I.

Introductory Collects.

I.

O LORD our God, of boundless might and incomprehensible glory, measureless compassion and infinite love to man, look down on us and on this holy house, and show unto us, and to them that pray with us, the riches of Thy mercies and compassions;* and so make us worthy, with a pure heart and a broken spirit, with hallowed lips and with a countenance that needeth not to be ashamed, to call upon Thee.†

II.

ALMIGHTY God, our heavenly Father, who hast promised that in all places where Thou dost record Thy name, Thou wilt meet with Thy servants to bless them; fulfil now Thy promise unto us, and make us joyful in

* S. Chrysostom (Neal's Oriental Liturgies).
† Liturgy of S. Mark.

Thine house of prayer; and grant that our worship, being offered in the name and in the Spirit of Thy Son, may be acceptable unto Thee and profitable unto ourselves; through our only Mediator and Advocate, Jesus Christ our Lord.*

III.

O GOD, light of the hearts that see Thee, and life of the souls that love Thee, and strength of the thoughts that seek Thee; from whom to be turned away is to fall, to whom to be turned is to rise, and in whom to abide is to stand fast for ever; grant us now Thy grace and blessing, as we are here assembled to offer up our common supplications; and though we are unworthy to approach Thee, or to ask anything of Thee at all, vouchsafe to hear and to answer us, for the sake of our great High Priest and Advocate, Jesus Christ our Lord.†

IV.

O GOD, our heavenly Father, who hast commanded men everywhere to pray and not to faint, and hast never said unto any, Seek ye my face in vain, help us by Thy good Spirit rightly to worship Thee. Hear us when

---

* Order of Public Worship, by Robert Lee, D.D.
† S. Augustine, chiefly.

we make unto Thee the confession of our sins. Hear us when we render unto Thee our thanksgiving for Thy mercies. Hear us when we ask of Thee such things as we need; and grant that those things which we ask faithfully we may obtain effectually, to the relief of our necessities and the setting forth of Thy glory;* through Jesus Christ our Lord.

V.

ALMIGHTY God, most merciful, most holy, full of compassion, ever ready to hear, and to answer them that call upon Thee, graciously hear us when we now present unto Thee our prayers and praises, through our only Mediator and Advocate, Jesus Christ our Lord. Call in our wandering thoughts: fix our affections on Thyself and on Thy service. May our worship be that which Thou desirest; and may our sacrifice be the sacrifice of a broken and a contrite spirit, with which Thou art ever well pleased.†

VI.

ALMIGHTY God, Father of lights, from whom cometh down every good and

* Anglican Liturgy, in part.
† Old Catholic Book of Devotion, chiefly.

perfect gift, grant unto Thy servants the spirit of grace and supplication, that we may draw near unto Thee now with humble, lowly, penitent, and obedient hearts, making confession of our great unworthiness, and asking of Thee such things as we need, for the worthiness of Thy Son, Jesus Christ our Lord.

VII.

O ALMIGHTY God, from whom every good prayer cometh, and who pourest out on all who desire it the spirit of grace and supplications, deliver us, when we draw nigh to Thee, from coldness of heart and wanderings of mind, that, with steadfast thoughts and kindled affections, we may worship Thee in spirit and in truth; through Jesus Christ our Lord.*

VIII.

O ETERNAL God, mighty in power, and of majesty incomprehensible, whom the heaven of heavens cannot contain, much less the walls of temples made with hands; to Thee alone be praise and adoration, from all the hosts of heaven, and all who dwell upon the earth; and as with joy and gratitude we are now assembled in this house, built to the honour of

* Bright's Ancient Collects.

Thy great name, send down upon us, we beseech Thee, Thy Holy Spirit, that we may lift up holy hands to Thee, and worship Thee with pure hearts. O God, who art from everlasting to everlasting, hear us, for the sake of Thy dear Son, Jesus Christ our Lord.*

IX.

O THOU who hast made Thy Church Thy dwelling-place, and chosen it as Thy rest for ever, and hast taught us in Thy Word not to forsake the assembling of ourselves together, regard in special mercy, we beseech Thee, all those who meet to-day in Thy holy courts. Manifest Thyself unto them as Thou dost not unto the world, and so bless unto them and to us all Thine ordinances, that our worship in the Church on earth may prepare us more fully for the blessed worship of Thy Church in heaven; through Jesus Christ our Lord.†

X.

O GOD, the Judge of all, who knowest what is in man, and requirest truth in the inward parts, mercifully grant that we may not draw near to Thee with our lips while our heart is far from Thee; and let Thy Holy Spirit help our infirmities, and pray with us and plead for

* German Reformed.   † Ibid.

us, that our offerings may be holy and well-pleasing unto Thee; through our great High Priest and perpetual Intercessor, Thy Son Jesus Christ.*

XI.

O GOD, the Father of our Lord God and Saviour Jesus Christ, ⌐whose name is great, whose nature is blissful, whose goodness is inexhaustible;⌐ Thou God and Master of all things, who art blessed for ever,⌐" who sittest on the cherubim, and art glorified by the seraphim," "before whom stand thousands of thousands and ten thousand times ten thousand, the hosts of holy angels and archangels;⌐ sanctify⌐O Lord,⌐ our souls and bodies and spirits,⌐and⌐touch our apprehensions,⌐and⌐search out our consciences, and cast out of us every evil thought,⌐ every base desire, all envy and pride and hypocrisy, all falsehood, all deceit, all worldly anxiety, all covetousness, vainglory, and sloth; all malice, all wrath, all anger, all remembrance of injuries, all blasphemy and every motion of the flesh and spirit that is contrary to Thy holy will;⌐ and so grant us, O Lord, grace with freedom, without condemnation, with a pure heart and a contrite soul, with sanctified lips, and without confusion of face, boldly to call upon Thee, our holy God and Father who art in heaven.†

---

* Manual of Prayers, Scudamore. † Liturgy of S. James.

XII.

LORD our God, great, eternal, wonderful in glory, who keepest covenant and promises for those that love Thee with their whole heart; [who art the Life of all, the Help of those that flee unto Thee, the Hope of those who cry unto Thee;] cleanse us from our sins, secret and open, and from every thought displeasing to Thy goodness; cleanse our bodies and souls, our hearts and consciences, that with a peaceful soul and a quiet mind, with perfect love and calm hope, we may venture confidently and fearlessly to pray unto Thee;* through Jesus Christ our Lord.

XIII.

HOLY, Most High, Awful, who dwellest in the holy place, make us holy, and bring us near to Thee, and cleanse us from all defilement, that we may perform the worship of our fathers in Thy fear, for Thou art He that blesses and hallows all things; through Jesus Christ our Lord.

* Coptic Liturgy of S. Basil.

II.

Confession of Sin.

I.

[Hear, O Lord, the humble confession of our sin.]

[*Instead of those connecting words, these from the* 1*st Epistle of S. John may be used:*—" If we say that we have no sin, we deceive ourselves, and the truth is not in us. If we confess our sins, He is faithful and just to forgive us our sins, and to cleanse us from all unrighteousness."]

O LORD our God, eternal and almighty Father, we acknowledge and confess before Thy holy Majesty that we are miserable sinners: born in iniquity, prone to evil: unable of ourselves to do that which is good: transgressing daily, and in many ways, Thy holy commandments, and by Thy just judgment deserving of condemnation and death. But, O Lord, we are deeply grieved for having offended

Thee. We condemn both ourselves and our sins with unfeigned penitence. We seek refuge in Thy mercy, and humbly entreat Thee to help us in our misery.

Be pleased, then, O Father of mercies, to have compassion on us, and for the sake of Jesus Christ Thy Son, to pardon all our sins. Grant unto us also, and increase in us from day to day, the grace of Thy Holy Spirit, that, acknowledging and bewailing more and more our iniquities, we may renounce them with all our hearts, and bring forth the fruits of righteousness, well-pleasing in Thy sight; through Jesus Christ our Lord.*

II.

[Hear, O Lord, the humble confession of our sin.]

WE are not worthy to come into Thy presence, by reason of our manifold offences. For we were conceived in sin, and in iniquity was every one of us born. All the days of our life we have continued to follow the corruption of our fleshly nature. If Thou, Lord, shouldest enter into judgment with Thy servants, just occasion hast Thou to punish, not only this our mortal flesh, but our bodies and souls for

* Confession of the Reformed Church.

ever. But Thou, O Lord, art a merciful God, a loving and favourable Father, to all that unfeignedly turn unto Thee from their sins; wherefore we most humbly beseech Thee, for the sake of Christ Thy Son, show Thy mercy upon us. Forgive us all our offences; endue us with Thy Holy Spirit; sanctify us wholly; and grant us Thy grace, that in all the days of our life hereafter we may study to serve and please Thee, in word and in deed; through our only Lord and Master, Jesus Christ.*

III.

[Hear, O Lord, the humble confession of our sin.]

WE have sinned against Thee, and have done wickedly. Our thoughts have been evil and vain continually. Our hearts have been deceitful above all things, and desperately wicked. Our members have been the instruments of unrighteousness to sin. We have not loved Thee with a pure heart fervently, neither have we loved our neighbour as ourselves. We have not done justly, or loved mercy, or walked humbly with Thee, our God. But we have been proud and envious, lustful and intemperate, greedy of sin and impatient

* John Knox.

of reproof, and Thee we have not glorified. We confess our sins before Thee: sins that are secret and sins that are open; sins that are forgotten and sins that are remembered, infinite in their degrees, intolerable in their load, we confess them all before Thee.*

Enter not into judgment with Thy servants, O Lord: for in Thy sight shall no flesh living be justified.†

Have mercy upon us, O Lord, according to Thy loving-kindness; according to the multitude of Thy tender mercies, blot out our iniquity.‡

Return, O Lord, how long? and let it repent Thee concerning Thy servants.§

Have pity on us, have pity on us according to Thy great mercy in Christ Jesus our Lord.

IV.

[Hear, O Lord, the humble confession of our sin.]

O ETERNAL, infinite, and almighty God, whose glory the heaven of heavens cannot contain, look down upon Thy unworthy servants, prostrate at the feet of Thy mercy, humbly confessing before Thee the sinfulness

---
* Various sources, chiefly Jeremy Taylor.
† Ps. cxliii. 2.   ‡ Ps. li. 1.   § Ps. xc. 13.

and vanity of their past lives, especially those sins which our consciences now charge against us, by which we have so greatly offended Thy Majesty and so grievously wounded our own souls.

We confess that we have sinned against Thee in thought, word, and deed, and are verily guilty in Thy sight. We acknowledge that we have not deserved the least of Thy mercies, but have deserved the greatest of Thy judgments. But Thou, O Lord, art full of mercy and compassion. Thou pardonest those that truly return to Thee; Thou restorest them that art penitent: wherefore we pray Thee, for Christ's sake, to grant unto us true repentance, and the aid of Thy Holy Spirit, that those things which we do at this present may please Thee, and that the rest of our life may be pure and holy, so that at the last we may come to Thine eternal joy; through Jesus Christ our Lord.*

V.

[Hear, O Lord, the humble confession of our sin.]

O GOD, Father of our Lord Jesus Christ, Maker of all things, Judge of all men, we acknowledge and bewail our manifold sins

---

* First part from old Book of Devotion, the last part adapted from Anglican Liturgy.

and wickedness, which we from time to time most grievously have committed, by thought, and word, and deed, against Thy divine Majesty, provoking most justly Thy wrath and indignation against us. We do earnestly repent, and are heartily sorry for these our misdoings. The remembrance of them is grievous unto us; the burden of them is intolerable. Have mercy upon us, have mercy upon us, most merciful Father, for Thy Son our Lord Jesus Christ's sake. Forgive us all that is past; and grant that we may hereafter serve and please Thee in newness of life, to the honour and glory of Thy name; through Jesus Christ our Lord.*

VI.

[Hear, O Lord, the humble confession of our sin.]

WE confess, O God, that we have sinned against Thee, and are unworthy of Thy mercy. We have not loved Thee, our Father; we have grieved the Holy Ghost, the earnest of our inheritance; we have not waited for the coming of Thy Son Jesus Christ our Lord; we have not been pure and holy; we have not been faithful and true; we have been entangled in the world, and overcome of evil.

* Anglican Liturgy.

We have lived in confusion and strife; we have done wrong unto our brother, and have not repented of the wrong; we have broken the unity of Thy holy Church, and caused men to forget and blaspheme Thy name. Our faith hath failed us; our love hath grown cold; our hope hath not been as an anchor entering within the vail. We remember these things before Thee; we cast ourselves upon Thy compassion; we cry unto Thee, Be merciful unto us, sinners. Hear us for the sake of Jesus Christ, who died for us upon the cross, and who rose again for our justification; that, obtaining of Thee forgiveness of all our sins, and being filled with Thy Holy Spirit, we may be enabled evermore to please Thee both in body and in soul.*

VII.

[Hear, O God, the humble confession of our sin.]

O GOD, searcher of hearts, in whom there is no darkness, and from whom our sins cannot be covered, we humble ourselves before Thy holy Majesty; we confess that we have been foolish, rebellious, deceived: we have been

---

* Various sources, chiefly from Liturgy and other Divine Offices of the Church (Catholic and Apostolic), commonly called "Irvingite."

unthankful for Thy mercies, distrustful of Thy promises, disobedient to Thy commands, and by our manifold wickedness have provoked Thee to cast us off from Thy favour and fellowship. Behold, we return unto Thee, our God, from whose ways we have so grievously departed, and implore Thy pardon for all our folly. Forgive us, we beseech Thee; forgive Thy people, whom Thou hast redeemed with the most precious blood of Thy dear Son; create in us clean and contrite hearts, and vouchsafe unto us Thy heavenly grace, that we turn not again unto folly; and give unto us heartily to forgive others, as we beseech Thee to forgive us, and to serve Thee henceforth in newness of life, to the glory of Thy holy name; through Jesus Christ our Lord.

VIII.

[Hear, O Lord, the humble confession of our sin.]

ALMIGHTY and most merciful Father, we have erred and strayed from Thy ways like lost sheep; we have followed too much the devices and desires of our own hearts; we have offended against Thy holy laws; we have left undone those things which we ought to have done, and we have done those things which we ought not to have done, and there is no health in us. But Thou, O Lord, have mercy upon us, miserable offenders. Spare Thou them, O God, which confess their faults; restore Thou them that are penitent, according to Thy promises declared unto mankind in Christ Jesus our Lord; and grant, O most merciful Father, for His sake, that we may hereafter live a godly, righteous, and sober life, to the glory of Thy holy name.*

IX.

[Hear, O Lord, the humble confession of our sin.]

ALMIGHTY and most merciful God, our heavenly Father, we cast ourselves down before Thee under a deep sense of our unworthiness and guilt. We have grievously sinned against Thee in thought, in word, and in deed; we have come short of Thy glory; we have broken Thy commandments and turned aside every one of us from the way of life, and in us there is no soundness nor health. Yet now, O most merciful Father, hear us when we call upon Thee with penitent hearts, and for the sake of Thy Son Jesus Christ have mercy upon us. Pardon our sins, and grant us Thy peace. Take away our guilt. Purify us by the inspiration of Thy Holy Spirit from all inward unclean-

* Anglican Liturgy.

ness, and make us able and willing to serve Thee in newness of life, to the glory of Thy holy name; through Jesus Christ our Lord.*

X.

[Hear, O Lord, the humble confession of our sin.]

THOU art truly good; we are altogether evil. Thou art holy; we are unholy. Thou art righteous; we are unrighteous. Thou art light; we are blind. Thou art life; we are dead. Thou art altogether truth; we are altogether vanity. Hear, O Father, the humble confession of our unworthiness. Thou who desirest not the death of a sinner, but rather that he should turn from his wickedness and live, suffer us not to perish in our sins. Thou who art the Saviour of the world, save us Thy servants. Thou teachest the ignorant; Thou soothest the sad; Thou forgivest the penitent. If we return Thou receivest; If we repent Thou sparest; even while we delay Thou art waiting. For Christ's sake pardon and forgive us. Make Thy grace sufficient for us; perfect Thy strength in our weakness. So we Thy people shall praise Thee, and evermore give thanks unto Thy name.†

* German Reformed. † Augustine, chiefly.

XI.

[Hear, O Lord, the humble confession of our sin.]

WE confess unto Thee, Father Almighty, Lord of heaven and earth, all our sins whatsoever which we have committed against Thee, and against the law of Christ. We confess unto Thee the desperate wickedness of our heart, out of which have proceeded all manner of evil thoughts and acts, for which things' sake Thy wrath is kindled against us, and we are without excuse before Thee this day. But especially, O God, with bitter contrition, we bewail those things which are the present burden of our heart and conscience. For all our sins and transgressions, our iniquities and offences, which in Thy grace Thou bringest to our remembrance, we abhor ourselves, and cast ourselves upon Thy mercy; and those which, through ignorance or carelessness, our foolishness, or the darkness of our heart through sin, we remember not nor think of, but which Thou, who knowest all secrets, seest that we have committed against Thee, do Thou forgive and cleanse us from them all, for Thy mercy's sake, O Lord. And accept our confession, and make our repentance sincere, through Jesus Christ our Lord.*

* Liturgy and other Offices of the Church (Catholic and Apostolic).

III.

Prayers for Pardon and Peace.

After Confession.

I.

ALMIGHTY God, the Father of our Lord Jesus Christ, who desirest not the death of a sinner, but rather that he may turn from his wickedness and live, and who pardonest and absolvest all them that truly repent, and unfeignedly believe Thy holy Gospel; we beseech Thee to grant us true repentance, and Thy Holy Spirit, that those things may please Thee which we do at this present; and that the rest of our life hereafter may be pure and holy, so that at the last we may come to Thine eternal joy; through Jesus Christ our Lord.

II.

IF any man sin, we have an advocate with the Father, Jesus Christ the righteous : and He is the propitiation for our sins.

As the heaven is high above the earth, so great is Thy mercy toward them that fear Thee.

Who is a God like unto Thee, who pardonest iniquity, and retainest not anger for ever; because Thou delightest in mercy?

We rejoice in Thy promises, O God: we hope in Thy word. Being justified freely by Thy grace, may we be made heirs, according to the hope of everlasting life. And having this hope in us, may we cleanse ourselves from all filthiness both of the flesh and of the spirit, and perfect holiness in Thy fear; that the peace of God, which passeth all understanding, may keep our hearts and minds; through Christ Jesus.*

III.

O WASH us thoroughly from our iniquity, and cleanse us from our sin; for we acknowledge our transgressions, and our sin is ever before us.

Be Thou merciful to our unrighteousness and our sins, and our iniquities do Thou remember no more.

Blot out our transgressions as a cloud, and as a thick cloud our sins, for we return unto Thee, because Thou hast redeemed us.

* Dr Lee's Order of Worship.

FOR PARDON AND PEACE.

Take away all our iniquity, and receive us graciously. Heal our backslidings, and love us freely. And let Thine anger be turned away from us, for in Thee the fatherless findeth mercy.

Though our sins be as scarlet, let them be white as snow; though they have been red as crimson, let them be as wool. Show Thy mercy on us, O Lord, and grant us Thy salvation.

O cast us not away from Thy presence, nor take Thy Holy Spirit away from us.*

IV.

ALMIGHTY God, the Father of our Lord Jesus Christ, who hath given us grace at this time to confess our sins unto Thee, for the sake of Jesus Christ, have mercy upon us. Grant unto us full remission and forgiveness, and absolve us from all our sins, iniquities, and transgressions; give unto us peace through the blessed Gospel of Thy dear Son, and vouchsafe unto us the inspiration of the Holy Spirit, that at this time present we may offer unto Thee true and acceptable worship, that for the time to come we may serve and please Thee in newness of life, in righteousness and true holiness; and that at the coming of our Lord Jesus Christ we may be found of Thee in peace unto salvation.

* From Scripture.

V.

O LORD, we beseech Thee, mercifully hear our prayers, and spare all them that confess their faults unto Thee; that they whose consciences by sin are accused, by Thy merciful pardon may be absolved; through Jesus Christ our Lord.

VI.

ALMIGHTY and everlasting God, who hatest nothing that Thou hast made, and dost forgive the sins of all them that are penitent; create and make in us new and contrite hearts, that we, worthily lamenting our sins, and acknowledging our wretchedness, may obtain of Thee, the God of all mercy, perfect remission and forgiveness; through Jesus Christ our Lord.*

VII.

RECEIVE our confession, O our only hope of salvation, through Jesus Christ our Lord. Thou who justifiest the ungodly, and quickenest the dead, justify and quicken us. Save us, O Lord and King of eternal glory, who canst save. O spare us and pity us, not

* Anglican.

according to our deserts, but according to Thy mercy. Cast not away, but receive us, according to Thy word, that we may live and not be disappointed of our hope ; and grant us Thy peace, which passeth understanding, now and evermore.*

* Gregorian.

IV.

Supplications.

I.

[Hear, O Lord, our humble supplications.]

WE beseech Thee to instruct us with Thy wisdom, to restrain us with Thy justice, to comfort us with Thy mercy, and to defend us by Thy power.*

Vouchsafe unto us the Sun of Righteousness; drive away all darkness from our hearts; lighten our eyes, that we sleep not unto death; and in Thy light may we see light.†

Give unto us true and perfect faith; give unto us the hearts of little children: may we be willing to believe where we cannot see, and willing to trust where we cannot comprehend.

Give unto us peace with Thee, our God; peace in our own souls, and, inasmuch as lieth in us, peace with all men.

* Catholic Book of Devotion.
† Daybreak Office of the Eastern Church.

SUPPLICATIONS.

Grant us, in all our duties, Thy help; in all our difficulties, Thy counsel; in all our dangers, Thy protection; and in all our sorrows, Thy peace.*

Take us into Thy keeping, both now and in the hour of death. Compass us about with Thy holy angels; cover us with the armour of Thy righteousness; fence us round about with Thy truth; make us faithful unto Thee upon the earth, and blessed with Thee in heaven.

II.

[Hear, O Lord, our humble supplications.]

MAKE us perfect in Christ Jesus: out of His fulness may we all receive, and rest in Him for evermore.

May His passion be our deliverance; His wounds, our healing; His cross, our redemption; and His death, our life.†

With His righteousness may we be clothed; by His Spirit may we be sanctified; in His blood may we be cleansed; and to His image may we be conformed.

May we be in Him as branches in the vine;

---

* Prayers for Social and Family Worship (Church of Scotland).
† Gelasian.

may He be in us the hope of glory, and unto us all in all.

May He be our Prophet to instruct us, our Priest to intercede for us, and our King to reign over us.

As He died, may we die unto sin; as He rose again, may we rise unto newness of life; suffering with Him here, may we reign with Him hereafter; and bearing now His cross, may we hereafter wear His crown.

III.

[Hear, O Lord, our humble supplications.]

SAVE us from the wicked thoughts of our minds, from the sinful desires of our hearts, and from the manifold temptations of our lives.*

Save us from those evils that we labour under now; from past evils that are the fruits of our many sins; and from evils to come that will be the just punishment of our offences.

Save us from all pain and misery, from all scandal and infamy, from evil diseases of soul and body, and from sudden and unforeseen death.†

From all blindness of heart; from pride,

---

* Catholic Book of Devotion. † Sarum Missal.

vainglory, and hypocrisy; from envy, hatred, and malice; and from all uncharitableness;

In all time of our tribulation, in all time of our wealth, in the hour of death, and in the day of judgment, good Lord, deliver us.*

IV.

[Hear, O Lord, our humble supplications.]

INCREASE in us the brightness of the Divine knowledge; impart to our thirsting souls the draught of life, and restore to our darkened minds the light of heaven.†

Make us to walk in purity and sincerity, to renounce the hidden things of dishonesty, and to have no fellowship with the works of darkness.‡

Grant us, O Lord, to mind not earthly things, but things heavenly; and, while placed among things that are passing away, to cleave unto those that abide for ever.§

Assist us to overcome all sensuality by self-denial; all selfishness by sacrifice; all anger by meekness; all indifference by devotion; and always evil with good.||

Deliver us from all earthly desires and carnal

---

* English Liturgy. † Mosarabic (Bright).
‡ Prayers for Social and Family Worship (Church of Scotland).
§ Leonine (Bright). || Catholic Book of Devotion.

appetites; amid the snares of a wicked world, protect our weakness with a never-failing love; and as by the necessity of nature we have borne the image of the earthly, so by the sanctification of grace may we bear the image of the heavenly and the pure.*

V.

[Hear, O Lord, our humble supplications.]

LET it be the work of our lives to obey Thee, the very joy of our souls to please Thee, and the satisfaction of our desires to dwell with Thee.

Make us children of quietness, and heirs of peace; kindle in us the fire of Thy love; plant in us the fear of Thy commandments; and strengthen our weakness by Thy power.†

Make us pure and sincere in speech, cheerful and zealous in duty, faithful in our several callings, and ready to every good work.

Make us prudent in our undertakings, temperate in all our enjoyments, patient in affliction, and humble in prosperity.

Suffer us not in health to forget Thee, or in sickness to think ourselves forgotten of Thee; and when the shadows of this life are passed

* Gelasian. † Syrian Clementine Liturgy.

away, may we enjoy the vision of Thy heavenly glory.*

VI.

[Hear, O Lord, our humble supplications.]

GRANT us to pass all the days of our life in peace and holiness, without sin and stumbling.

Enable us to perform our allotted tasks with diligence, to guide our affairs with prudence and discretion, and in all our ways to acknowledge Thee.

Feed us with food convenient for us; bestow upon us health of body and soundness of mind; and further our lawful undertakings with Thy blessing.

Restrain us from all intemperance and excess, from all vanity in speech and behaviour; and make us sober and watchful to prayer.

Repress in us all inordinate desires after earthly riches: keep us from coveting that which is not ours; and having food and raiment, may we be content.

Discover to us the nothingness of this world, the exceeding greatness of the world to come, the nearness of death, and judgment, and eternity.†

---
* Catholic Book of Devotion.
† Prayers for Social and Family Worship (Church of Scotland).

VII.

[Hear, O Lord, our humble supplications.]

BIND us closely to Thee and to each other in one firm and indissoluble bond of unity.

May our conversation be edifying, our influence in the world for good; and may our light so shine before others that they may come to glorify Thee.

Grant us that charity which covereth a multitude of sins; that love which is the fulfilling of the law; the unity of the Spirit, and the bond of peace.

Preserve us from all hurtful and passionate actions, from all rashness and bitterness of speech: may we love our friends in Thee, and our enemies for Thy sake.*

Make us kindly affectioned one to another, and ready to bear the burdens of the weak; willing to distribute, ready to communicate.

Deliver us from love of self and indifference to others: forgive us all the evil we have done them; condemn us not for the good we have omitted to do them. Direct our life in good works; and, after our passage through this world, vouchsafe us eternal rest with the righteous.†

* Mosarabic. † Ibid.

VIII.

[Hear, O Lord, our humble supplications.]

IN Thy mercy and majesty behold Thy household, that they may neither be stained with vices of their own, nor held in bondage by the sins of others; but that, being ever freed from both, they may do service unto Thee.*

Fill us with such love to Thee that nothing may be too hard to do, or too grievous to suffer, for Thy sake. In our prosperity and adversity may we alike be Thine: may joy without Thee be sorrow, and may sorrow for Thee be joy.†

Let the brightness of Thy Spirit illumine our renewed souls, that He may kindle our cold hearts and light up our dark minds; that He may fill us with heavenly desires, and purify us from every stain.‡

Grant that without terror we may await the peaceful coming of Jesus Christ our Lord; that He may find us not sleeping in our sins, but awake and rejoicing in His praises: that we may go forth undefiled to meet Him in the company of His saints, and may be found worthy of the banquet of eternal life.§

* Leonine. † Augustine.
‡ Gothic. § Gelasian.

IX.

[Hear, O Lord, our humble supplications.]

O LORD, make us poor in spirit: that ours may be the kingdom of heaven.

Make us to mourn for sin: that we may be comforted by Thy grace.

Make us meek, O Lord: that we may inherit the earth.

Make us to hunger and thirst after righteousness: that we may be filled therewith.

Make us merciful, O Lord: that we may obtain mercy.

Make us pure in heart: that we may see Thee, our God.

Make us peacemakers: that we may be called the children of God.

Make us willing to be persecuted for righteousness' sake: that our reward may be in heaven.

X.

[Hear, O Lord, our humble supplications.]

TAKE from us that carnal mind which is death, and increase in us ever more and more that spiritual mind which is life and peace.

Give us earnestness, strength of purpose, simplicity of faith, warmth of love.

Make us kindly in thought; gentle in word; generous in deed.

Teach us that it is better to give than to receive; better to forget ourselves than to put ourselves forward; better to minister than to be ministered unto; better to be last than to be first.

Preserve and keep us in the constant sense of our membership of Christ; in the unfailing thought that we are His soldiers and servants; in the love of our Father's house; and in the hope of our eternal home.

May we live by faith in Christ; may we increase in union with Him; may we this day and every day become more and more like Him, till we see Him as He is, and be changed into His perfect likeness.*

XI.

[Hear, O Lord, our humble supplications.]

TEACH us day by day what Thou wouldest have us to do, and give us grace and power to fulfil the same.

Enlighten our understandings, that we may know Thee; sanctify our affections, that we

* Alford.

may love Thee; and put Thy fear into our hearts, that we may dread to offend Thee.*

We renounce the works of darkness; cause us to walk in the light of Thy countenance. We renounce the vanities of this world; help us to seek after the enduring substance laid up with Thee in heaven. We renounce the sinful lusts of the flesh; enable us to walk in the Spirit.†

Strengthen us by Thy grace, that the same holy faith which we own with our tongues, we may confess in the innocency of our lives.

Keep us from harm within and without; from the evil in the world around us; from the evil that is within ourselves; from the Evil One who lies in wait for our souls.‡

Give us an healthful body, a pure and holy soul, a sanctified and humble spirit; and preserve body, soul, and spirit harmless unto the coming of the Lord Jesus.§

XII.

[Hear, O Lord, our humble supplications.]

GIVE us, O Lord, so to know Christ and His life, that the same mind which was in Him may be in us; that we may be in the world as He was in the world.

---

* German Reformed.   † Ibid.   ‡ Alford.
§ German Reformed.

Give us, O Lord, so to know Christ and His death, that we may not glory save in His cross ; whereby the world is crucified unto us, and we unto the world.

Give us, O Lord, so to know Christ, and the power of His resurrection, that, like as He was raised from the dead by the glory of the Father, we also may walk in newness of life.

Give us, O Lord, so to know Christ and His ascension, that our conversation may be in heaven ; and that we may seek those things that are above, where He sitteth at Thy right hand.

Give us, O Lord, so to know Christ and His second coming, that our lamps may be burning and our loins girt about, and we ourselves as servants waiting for their master.

Give us, O Lord, so to know Christ as Judge of quick and of dead, that we may give in our account with joy, and may be welcomed by Him to the kingdom of the Father.

XIII.

[Hear, O Lord, our humble supplications.]

LET Thy grace, which hath appeared unto us, and unto all men, bringing salvation, teach us to deny all ungodliness and worldly lusts, and to live soberly, righteously, and godly in this present world.

Let our wisdom be not that which is from beneath, which is earthly, sensual, devilish; but that which is from above, which is first pure, then peaceable, gentle, easy to be entreated, without partiality, and without hypocrisy.

Teach us to endure hardness as good soldiers of Jesus Christ, that we may not fear the reproach of men, nor be ashamed of Christ or of His Cross; and that we may not count life itself dear unto us, so we may finish our course with joy.

Quicken us to work the works of Him that hath sent us while it is day, because the night cometh wherein no man can work; and what we do, enable us to do it heartily, as unto the Lord, and not unto men.

Keep us all the days of our appointed time till our change comes; and when we walk through the valley of the shadow of death, be Thou with us, that we may fear no evil; and hereafter may we dwell in the house of the Lord for ever.*

* From Scripture.

V.

Prayers,

With which any of the foregoing may be concluded.

I.

ALMIGHTY Father, who art the hearer of prayer, unto whom all flesh shall come, be pleased to pardon what has been amiss in this our service. Forgive our wandering and unholy thoughts; forgive our rash and presumptuous words: accept of us, and accept of our offering, and let Thy blessing be upon us for evermore; through Jesus Christ our Lord.

Amen.

II.

O THOU who bestowest liberally and upbraidest not, be pleased now, for Thy Son's sake, to give unto us those things which we have asked in His name, and to forgive our unworthiness in asking. Evermore pardon all our sins ; deliver us from all evils, past, present, and to come ; preserve us in the faith and fear of Thy holy name unto our life's end, and bring us at last into Thine heavenly kingdom; through Jesus Christ our Lord.*

Amen.

III.

O GOD, who forsakest not them that trust in Thee, mercifully hear our prayers ; and since our weakness is such that we can do nothing without Thee, grant us the assistance of Thy grace, that with Thee we may do all things, and serve Thee acceptably ; through Jesus Christ our Lord.†

Amen.

IV.

HEAR, O Lord, these our supplications ; pardon their sinfulness and imperfection. Give unto us those things that are good for us to receive of Thee ; keep from us those things that are evil ; lead us into all truth and righteousness, and bring us to Thine eternal kingdom ; through Jesus Christ our Lord.

Amen.

* Jeremy Taylor, chiefly.   † Anglican Liturgy.

V.

ALMIGHTY God, the fountain of all wisdom, who knowest our necessities before we ask, and our ignorance in asking, we beseech Thee to have compassion upon our infirmities; and those things which for our unworthiness we dare not, and for our blindness we cannot ask, vouchsafe to give us, for the worthiness of Thy Son, Jesus Christ our Lord.*

Amen.

VI.

ALMIGHTY and everlasting God, who art always more ready to hear than we to pray, and art wont to give more than either we desire or deserve; pour down upon us the abundance of Thy mercy; forgiving us those things whereof our conscience is afraid, and giving us those good things which we are not worthy to ask but through the merits and mediation of Jesus Christ Thy Son, our Lord.†

Amen.

VII.

GIVE ear, O Lord, unto the voice of those who have now offered up their prayers unto Thee; reject not the unworthy supplica-

* Anglican Liturgy.   † Ibid.

tions of Thy servants; but grant us the blessings we have asked, and all other things necessary for us, in the name of Jesus Christ our Lord; unto whom, with the Father and the Holy Ghost, be honour and praise for ever.*

Amen.

VIII.

ALMIGHTY God, who hast given us grace at this time with one accord to make our common supplications unto Thee, and dost promise that when two or three are gathered together in Thy name, Thou wilt grant their requests; fulfil now, O Lord, the desires and petitions of Thy servants, as may be most expedient for them; granting us in this world knowledge of Thy truth, and in the world to come life everlasting.†

Amen.

IX.

ALMIGHTY God, who hast promised to hear the petitions of them that ask in Thy Son's name; we beseech Thee mercifully to incline Thine ears to us that have made now our prayers and supplications unto Thee, and grant that those things which we have faith-

* Liturgy of Neuchâtel.   † S. Chrysostom.

fully asked, according to Thy will, may effectually be obtained, to the relief of our necessity, and to the setting forth of Thy glory; through Jesus Christ our Lord.*

Amen.

X.

RECEIVE, O Lord, with compassionate kindness, the prayers of Thy suppliant people, and bestow upon them plenteously the aids of Thy heavenly grace, that they may both know what things they ought to do, and be strong also to do what they know; through Jesus Christ our Lord, who liveth and reigneth with Thee and the Holy Ghost, ever one God, world without end.

Amen.

XI.

O GOD, all righteous and all holy, before whom the highest angels stand charged with folly, regard not, we beseech Thee, the infirmities by which our prayers are marred, but in Thy mercy accept and answer them, through Jesus Christ, the only sacrifice and propitiation for mankind.

Amen.

* Anglican.

XII.

WE humbly entreat Thee, most merciful God, to receive graciously the sacrifices of praise and prayer which we this day offer unto Thee.

Let the cry of Thy family enter into Thine ears, O Father: and send unto Thy children an answer in peace; through our Elder Brother Jesus Christ, who is also our High Priest and Sacrifice, and the altar which sanctifieth our gift; and to whom, with Thee and the Holy Ghost, be all glory in the Church, for ever and ever.

Amen.

VI.

Thanksgiving.

I.

[Hear, O Lord, our thanksgiving for Thy mercy.]
[*Instead of these, the following words may be used* (51*st Ps.*) :—" O Lord, open Thou our lips ; and our mouth shall show forth Thy praise."]

O GOD, Thy glory is great in all the Churches, and the praises of Thy name resound in the assemblies of Thy saints. We, Thy servants, would humble ourselves before Thee: we worship Thine infinite majesty ; we celebrate Thy wisdom, power, and goodness, that shine forth in the works of creation and redemption, through Jesus Christ our Lord ; we bless Thee for all temporal and spiritual good that we continually receive at Thy bountiful hands ; but more especially, with all Thy people assembled this day we praise Thee that Thou didst send into the world Thy Son to save us; and, having delivered Him for our offences, didst raise Him up again for our justification, and through His glorious resurrection hast given us the blessed hope of everlasting life.

O Lord, may these our thanksgivings come up with acceptance before Thy throne. Make us worthy at the last day to have part in the resurrection of the just, and the glory of the kingdom of heaven, whither Jesus the Forerunner is for us entered; where now He lives and reigns, and is worshipped and glorified with Thee and the Holy Ghost, God blessed for ever.*

II.

[Hear, O Lord, our thanksgiving for Thy mercy.]

WE render unto Thee our thanksgiving, O Father of mercies, for all Thy goodness unto us. We bless Thee that Thou hast spared us hitherto, and brought us to the worship of Thy holy name; that Thou hast preserved us safe amidst the chances and changes of this mortal life, and hast supplied our wants out of Thy fulness. But especially we bless Thee for sending Thy Son, Jesus Christ, into

* Liturgy of the Reformed Church.

the world to lighten our darkness, and lead us unto heavenly truth. We bless Thee for His holy incarnation, for His life on earth, for His precious sufferings and death upon the cross, for His resurrection from the dead, for His glorious ascension to Thy right hand, whence He shall come again to judge the quick and the dead. We bless Thee for the giving of the Holy Ghost, for all the sacraments and ordinances of Thy Church, for the communion of saints, for the forgiveness of sins, for the resurrection of the body, and for the life everlasting. Thee, mighty God, heavenly King, we magnify and praise. With angels and archangels, and with all the company of heaven, we laud and magnify Thy glorious name: evermore praising Thee, and saying, Holy, holy, holy, Lord God of Hosts; heaven and earth are full of Thy glory: glory be to Thee, O Lord most high.

III.

[Hear, O Lord, our thanksgiving for Thy mercy.]

WE praise and bless Thy holy name, Father of mercies and God of all grace, that Thou hast had compassion upon us, miserable sinners: that Thou didst send Thy Son to seek and save us: that He took on Him the form of a servant, and the likeness of sinful flesh, and fulfilled Thy law, and was obedient to all Thy will, even unto death: that He made propitiation for our sins: and when He had overcome the sharpness of death, He opened the kingdom of heaven to all believers: that He sitteth at Thy right hand in glory everlasting: that He will come again in majesty to judge the quick and the dead: and will reign till all enemies are put under His feet: that He is our Advocate with Thee, the Captain of our salvation, the Author and Finisher of the faith: that He is our light, and life, and hope: that He is not untouched with the feeling of our infirmities, having been in all points tempted as we are: that He ever liveth to make intercession, and saveth to the uttermost them that come unto Thee by Him: That Thou hast sent unto us the gospel of Thy grace; and hast permitted us to enjoy another of the days of the Son of man upon the earth, to unite with Thy Church militant in calling upon Thy name, and learning the way of that eternal life,* which is in the knowledge of Thee, and of Him whom Thou hast sent, our Lord and Saviour Jesus Christ.

* Order of Public Worship, by Robert Lee, D.D.

IV.

[Hear, O Lord, our thanksgiving for Thy mercy.]

ALMIGHTY God, who, dwelling in the highest heaven, vouchsafest to regard the lowest creature upon earth, we humbly adore, and, with all the powers of our soul, praise Thy holy name for all the blessings Thou hast bestowed upon us. We bless Thee for electing us in Thy favour, creating us in Thine image, redeeming us by Thy Son, and sanctifying us by Thy Spirit; for preserving us amid all the changes and encounters of this life, and raising up our thoughts to the hope of a better life to come.* May we love Thee as Thou hast loved us; as we have been redeemed by Thy mercy, may we dedicate ourselves to Thy service, that we who have received from Thee things that are holy and blessed, may be ourselves holy and blessed for evermore.

V.

[Hear, O Lord, our thanksgiving for Thy mercy.]

ALMIGHTY God, Father of all mercies, we, Thine unworthy servants, do give Thee most humble and hearty thanks for all

* Catholic Book of Devotion.

Thy goodness and loving-kindness to us and to all men. We bless Thee for our creation, preservation, and all the blessings of this life; but, above all, for Thine inestimable love in the redemption of the world by our Lord Jesus Christ, for the means of grace, and for the hope of glory; and we beseech Thee, give us that due sense of all Thy mercies, that our hearts may be unfeignedly thankful, and that we may show forth Thy praise, not only with our lips, but in our lives, by giving up ourselves to Thy service, and by walking before Thee in holiness and righteousness all our days; through Jesus Christ our Lord.*

VI.

[Hear, O Lord, our thanksgiving for Thy mercy.]

ALMIGHTY God, Father of mercies, the fountain of comfort and blessing, life and peace, plenty and pardon, who fillest heaven with Thy glory and earth with Thy goodness; we give Thee most humble thanks for Thy goodness unto us Thy servants in our several estates and conditions; refreshing us with Thy comforts, enlarging us with Thy blessing, preserving us from all accident and calamity, sickness and death; lightening our afflictions and

* Anglican Liturgy.

healing our sorrows; and, in the multitude of Thy mercies, bringing us into Thine house of prayer with a song of thanksgiving. For all Thy bounties known to us, for all unknown, we give Thee thanks; but chiefly that when, through disobedience, we had fallen from Thee, thou didst not suffer us to depart from Thee for ever; but hast ransomed us from eternal death, and given us the joyful hope of everlasting life, through Jesus Christ our Lord.

We praise Thee, O Lord, we bless Thy name for ever and ever. Every day will we bless Thee, and we will praise Thy name for ever and ever. Not unto us, O Lord, not unto us, but to Thy name be the glory and the praise, for Thy mercy and Thy truth's sake. Henceforth and for evermore we will praise Thy holy name.

VII.

[Hear, O Lord, our thanksgiving for Thy mercy.]

WE render thanks unto Thy name, O God most High; for Thou hast created us in Thine own image; Thou hast given us souls to know and love Thee; Thou hast made us a little lower than the angels; Thou hast supplied all our wants; Thou hast loaded us with Thy benefits; Thou hast caused our cup to run over. We have sinned against Thee; but Thou hast spared us: we have wandered from Thee; but Thou hast sought us: we were lost; but Thou hast saved us. O God our Saviour, Thou hast broken our chains, that we might be free; Thou hast healed our diseased souls, that we might not perish; Thou hast enriched us who were poor with the treasures of Thy salvation; Thou hast made us who had nothing to inherit all things; and even now, all things are ours. Therefore, with one heart and with one voice we laud and magnify Thy glorious name; and, with Thy saints on earth and in heaven, we ascribe blessing, and honour, and glory, and power, unto Him that sitteth upon the throne, and unto the Lamb, for ever and ever.*

VIII.

[Hear, O Lord, our thanksgiving for Thy mercy.]

IT is a good thing to give thanks unto Thee, O God, to show forth Thy loving-kindness in the morning, and Thy faithfulness every night. We thank Thee for all the bounties of Thy providence: for health and strength, food and raiment; for help and succour in times

* Chiefly Order of Public Worship, by Robert Lee, D.D.

of need, for pity and consolation in times of sorrow; and for all the kindness Thou hast shown us from the beginning of our days until now. But above all, we thank Thee for Thine infinite love to us, miserable and unworthy; that Thou hast given Thy Son to be the propitiation for our sins; that Thou hast given Thy Holy Spirit to sanctify our corrupt natures; that Thou hast called us out of darkness into the marvellous light of Thy Gospel; that Thou hast favoured us with the means of grace, and hast comforted our souls with the hope of immortal glory; and do Thou help us, we beseech Thee, more worthily to acknowledge Thy goodness, in all time to come, by trusting more entirely in Thee, by fuller contentment with the portion Thou hast given us, by greater charity towards others, and by a more strict obedience to Thy holy commandments.

IX.

[Hear, O Lord, our thanksgiving for Thy mercy.]

IN goodness art Thou exalted, O Lord, our Father, for ever and ever. We magnify Thee, we praise Thee, we worship Thee, we give thanks unto Thee for Thy bountiful providence; for all the blessings of the present life, and all the hopes of a better life to come. Let the memory of Thy goodness, we beseech Thee, fill our hearts with joy and thankfulness unto our life's end; and let no unworthiness of ours provoke Thee to withhold from us any needed good, seeing that all Thy blessings come not by our desert, but only through the merit and mediation of Jesus Christ our Lord.*

X.

[Hear, O Lord, our thanksgiving for Thy mercy.]

O GOD, giver of all good and fountain of all mercies; in whom are the springs of our life: all glory, thanks, and praise be unto Thee for thine ever-flowing goodness; for Thy faithfulness, which is from one generation to another; for Thy mercies, which are new every morning, fresh every moment, and more than we can number; for seed-time and harvest, and summer and winter, and nights and days throughout the year; for food and raiment and shelter; for health and reason; for childhood and age, and youth and manhood; for Thy fatherly hand ever upon us in sickness and in health, in joy and in sorrow, in life and in death;

* German Reformed.

for friends and kindred and kind benefactors; for home and country; for Thy Church and for Thy Gospel. Yea, Lord, for that there is nothing for which we may not bless and thank Thee, therefore do we call upon Thy name, and pay our vows now in the presence of all Thy people, humbly beseeching Thee to accept our service, even as we offer it in the name and through the infinite merits of Thy Son Jesus Christ, our Lord.*

* German Reformed.

VII.

Prayers for Illumination.

I.

O GOD, with whom is the well of life, and in whose light we see light; shed into all the faculties of our soul the brightness of Thy divine knowledge ; and give us to drink of the rivers of Thy pleasure, that our thirsting souls may not be near the living water without drinking of it, nor our minds remain in darkness when the light from heaven is around us.

II.

O LORD and Lover of men, cause the pure light of Thy divine knowledge to shine forth in our hearts, and open the eyes of our understandings, that we may comprehend the precepts of Thy Gospel. Plant in us also the fear of Thy blessed commandments ; that, trampling upon all carnal appetites, we may seek a heavenly citizenship, both saying and doing always such things as shall please Thee.*

III.

O LORD God our Sun, by whom light is sown to the righteous and gladness for the upright in heart, illuminate our minds, we beseech Thee, by Thy heavenly grace, and fill them with the pure wisdom which cometh from above, that we may walk before Thee in simplicity and godly sincerity all our days; not taking counsel of the world or of the flesh, but aiming and endeavouring in all things only to know and do Thy will, through Jesus Christ our Lord.

IV.

ALMIGHTY God, by whose inspiration all Holy Scripture hath been given, grant us grace to love Thy Word fervently, to search the Scriptures diligently, to read them humbly, to understand them truly, and to live after them effectually, and so by them to order our lives that we may be always acceptable unto Thee.

* Liturgy of S. Chrysostom.

V.

O LORD, who alone canst give the hearing ear and the understanding heart ; open our minds, we beseech Thee, to understand Thy Word, which Thou hast in Thy mercy bestowed upon us. Save us from using Thy Word deceitfully ; from wresting it to serve our own purpose ; from being in bondage to the letter while we neglect its spirit. But grant that we may search the Scriptures diligently, and find in them their testimony to Christ; and beholding His glory reflected in them, may be changed into it ever more and more, till we are made like Him in His heavenly kingdom, through the same Jesus Christ our Lord.*

VI.

ALMIGHTY God, who hast begotten us with Thy Word, renewed us with Thy Spirit, fed us with Thy sacraments and with the daily ministry of Thine appointment, still go on to build us up unto life everlasting. Let Thy blessing rest upon us in reading and hearing Thy holy Word, that we may do so humbly and reverently, with a mind desirous both to hear and to obey ; that so we may be furnished unto

* Mosarabic.

every good word and work, and enabled to keep Thy holy commandments to the glory of Thy name.*

VII.

O GOD, without whom Paul may plant and Apollos water, but from whom alone cometh the increase; grant this increase unto us; that we may speak that which we believe, and may hear as those who listen to that Gospel according to which they have yet to be judged.

VIII.

O GOD, who hast promised that in the last days the mountain of the Lord's house shall be exalted above the hills, and all nations shall flow unto it; send forth Thy light and Thy truth now unto Thy servants; leading them in the paths of Thine ordinances, and in the ways of Thy commandments; that Thy whole Church, perfect in every member, complete in holiness and instructed in righteousness, may be presented before Thee without spot or blemish, in the day of the appearing and kingdom of the Lord Jesus.

* Jeremy Taylor, chiefly.

IX.

LET Thy Gospel, O Lord, come unto us not in word only but in power, and in much assurance, and in the Holy Ghost, that we may be guided unto all truth, and strengthened unto all obedience and enduring of Thy will with joyfulness; that, abounding in the work of faith and the labour of love and the patience of hope, we may finally be made meet to be partakers of the inheritance of the saints in light; through Jesus Christ our Lord.*

X.

O LORD Jesus Christ, who at Thy first coming didst send Thy messenger to prepare Thy way before Thee, grant that the ministers and stewards of Thy mysteries may likewise so prepare and make ready Thy way, by turning the hearts of the disobedient to the wisdom of the just; that at Thy second coming, to judge the world, we may be found an acceptable people in Thy sight, who livest and reignest with the Father and the Holy Spirit, ever one God, world without end.†

* Order of Public Worship, by Robert Lee, D.D.
† Anglican Liturgy.

XI.

ALMIGHTY God, with whom are hid all the treasures of wisdom and knowledge, open our eyes, that we may behold wondrous things out of Thy law, and give us grace that we may clearly understand and heartily choose the way of Thy commandments; through Jesus Christ our Lord.*

XII.

O GOD, whose inspiration giveth understanding, and who didst bestow upon Thy servants of old gifts of wisdom, and knowledge, and utterance; be pleased so to guide and direct the hearts and lips of us, Thy servants, who are here assembled before Thee, that our speaking and hearing may be to our satisfaction and profit; to the increase of our knowledge, and faith, and obedience; and to our comfort and growth in grace; through Jesus Christ our Lord.

* Prayers for Social and Family Worship (Church of Scotland).

VIII.

Ascriptions of Praise,

With which the Sermon may be ended.

I.

BLESSING, and honour, and glory, and power be unto Him that sitteth upon the throne, and unto the Lamb for ever and ever.
Amen.

II.

NOW unto the King eternal, immortal, invisible, the only wise God, be honour and glory for ever and ever.
Amen.

III.

NOW unto Him that is able to do exceeding abundantly, above all that we ask or think, according to the power that worketh in

us; unto Him be glory in the Church by Christ Jesus, throughout all ages, world without end.
Amen.

IV.

NOW unto Him that is able to keep us from falling, and to present us faultless before the presence of His glory with exceeding joy; to the only wise God our Saviour, be glory and majesty, dominion and power, both now and ever.
Amen.

V.

UNTO Him that loved us, and washed us from our sins in His own blood, and hath made us kings and priests unto God, His Father; to Him be glory and dominion for ever and ever.
Amen.

VI.

NOW unto the blessed and only Potentate, the King of kings and Lord of lords, who only hath immortality, dwelling in the light which no man can approach unto, whom no man hath seen or can see, to Him be honour and power everlasting.
Amen.

VII.

NOW unto the God of all grace, who hath called us unto His eternal glory by Christ Jesus, be glory and dominion for ever and ever.

          Amen.

VIII.

GLORY be to the Father, and to the Son, and to the Holy Ghost; as it was in the beginning, is now, and ever shall be, world without end.

 Amen.

IX.

Prayers after Sermon.

I.

O GOD, who hast sounded in our ears Thy divine and saving oracles; enlighten the souls of us sinners to the full understanding of what has been spoken; that we may not only be hearers of spiritual words, but doers of good works; following after faith unfeigned, blameless life, and conduct without reproach; through Jesus Christ our Lord.*

II.

GRANT, we beseech Thee, Almighty God, that the words which we have heard this day with our outward ears may, through Thy grace, be so grafted inwardly in our hearts, that they may bring forth in us the fruit of good living, to the honour and praise of Thy name; through Jesus Christ our Lord.†

* Liturgy of S. James. † Anglican Liturgy.

III.

O GOD, who didst teach the hearts of Thy faithful people by sending to them the light of Thy Holy Spirit, grant unto us, by the same Spirit, to have a right understanding of Thy saving truth ; visit, we pray Thee, this congregation with Thy love and favour ; enlighten their minds more and more with the light of the everlasting Gospel ; graft in their hearts a love of the truth ; increase in them true religion ; nourish them with all goodness, and of Thy great mercy keep them in the same ; through Jesus Christ our Lord.*

IV.

O MERCIFUL God, the comforter and teacher of Thy faithful people, we most humbly beseech Thee to give us grace not only to be hearers of the word, but doers also of the same ; not only to love, but also to live Thy gospel ; not only to favour, but also to follow Thy godly doctrine ; not only to profess, but also to practise Thy blessed commandments ; that whatsoever we outwardly hear, or inwardly believe, we may show forth the same in our conversation and life, unto the honour of Thy holy

* German Reformed Liturgy.

name, the comfort of our brethren, and the health of our own souls;* through Jesus Christ our Lord.

V.

O THOU who wilt manifest Thy glory in the gathering in of Thy saints, grant to us that we, having received the good seed of Thine engrafted word, may thereby grow up unto Thee, and, becoming ripened for Thine harvest, may, in the last great day, be gathered by Thine angels into Thine heavenly garner. Keep us from the snares of the Wicked One, from the snares of the ungodly world, and from the evil that is in our own hearts, and preserve Thou us pure and clean unto the day of Thy coming; and then, O Lord, be Thou glorified in us, and make us to behold Thy glory among them that shall shine as the sun in the kingdom of the Father.†

VI.

O GOD, who hast revealed to us the light of Thy gospel, and called us into the fellowship of Thy Son Jesus Christ, grant that we may put away the works of darkness, and may walk in purity, uprightness, and sincerity, that

* Becon.   † Beza.

we may have fellowship with Thee, for Thou art light, and with Thee there is no darkness at all; that, when the shadows of this mortal life are passed away, we may behold those things which the eye of man hath not seen, and be made partakers of everlasting glory; through Jesus Christ our Lord.*

VII.

O GOD, whose Word is quick and powerful, and sharper than a two-edged sword, grant unto us who are here before Thee, and to all Thy people everywhere, that we may receive Thy truth into our hearts in faith and love. By it may we be taught and guided, upheld and comforted; that we be no longer children in understanding, but grow to the stature of perfect men in Christ Jesus, and prepared to every good word and work, to the honour of Thy name; through our Lord and Saviour Jesus Christ.†

VIII.

SUFFER not, O God, the good seed which the Son of man hath sown to be caught away by the wicked one out of our hearts, or to be scorched by tribulation or persecution, or to be

---

* Order of Public Worship, by Robert Lee, D.D.   † Ibid.

choked with cares and pleasures of this life ; but, being received into good and honest hearts, may it bring forth in us abundantly the fruits of faith and obedience ; through our Lord and Saviour Jesus Christ.*

* Order of Public Worship, by Robert Lee, D.D.

X.

Intercessions.

I.

1.

O GOD, who hast taught us to make prayers and supplications for all men, and first for those in authority, we entreat Thee to bless all princes and governors, Thy servants, to whom Thou hast committed the administration of justice, and to grant them the daily increase of Thy good Spirit, that, with true faith acknowledging Thy Son, our Saviour, to be King of kings and Lord of lords, they may serve Thee, exalt Thy rule in their dominions, and so govern their subjects that Thy people everywhere, being kept in peace and quietness, may serve Thee in all godliness and honesty.

Especially we beseech Thee thus to bless our Sovereign Lady Queen Victoria, and to give her grace so to execute her office that religion may be maintained, manners reformed, and sin punished, according to Thy Word.

Make Thy blessing also to rest upon Albert Edward, Prince of Wales, the Princess of Wales, and all the members of the Royal Family.

Grant a spirit of wisdom and of the fear of the Lord to the Queen's counsellors, to the nobles, rulers, and judges of the realm [and to the members of Parliament at this time assembled]; preside in their councils, and so direct all their deliberations that they may promote Thy glory and the public good.

We pray for the prosperity of this empire and all its dependencies; for favourable weather, plenteous harvests, and peaceful times; for a blessing on our fleets and armies, our trade and commerce, and upon every useful and honest occupation.

2.

ALMIGHTY God, King of saints, who hast chosen Zion for Thy habitation and Thy rest for ever, we pray Thee for all whom Thou hast appointed pastors and ministers in Thy Church, and particularly for him [those] to whom Thou hast given the charge of this flock. Animate them with Thy Spirit, that they may fulfil their ministry with fidelity and zeal, and labour effectually for the conversion and salvation of souls. Send forth faithful labourers into

Thy harvest, and for this end give Thy grace to those who are preparing to serve Thee in the holy ministry, and bless their studies. Send down the healthful influences of Thy Spirit upon all schools and seminaries of learning, and cause to reign in them that fear of Thy name which is the beginning of wisdom.

We beseech Thee on behalf of the Church universal, that it may please Thee to protect it everywhere, and to increase and sanctify it more and more; to remove the errors, scandals, and divisions which desolate it, and to reunite all Christians in the bonds of truth, piety, and peace. Particularly we commend to Thee this parish, beseeching Thee to bless all the families and individuals of which it is composed, and to cause all the Christian virtues to flourish among them. And forasmuch as Thou wouldst be known as the Saviour of all mankind in the redemption procured by Thy Son Jesus Christ, grant that such as are still strangers to the knowledge of Thee, and plunged in the darkness of ignorance and error, may be illuminated by the light of Thy Gospel, and led into the right way of salvation, which is to know Thee the only true God, and Jesus Christ whom Thou hast sent; and may those whom Thou hast already visited with Thy grace grow daily in godliness, and be enriched more and more with spiritual gifts, that we all with one heart may adore Thee as our Creator and Father, and submit ourselves to Jesus Christ Thy Son as our Redeemer and King.

3.

GOD of all comfort, we commend to Thy mercy all those whom Thou art pleased to visit with any cross or tribulation ; the nations whom Thou dost afflict with famine, pestilence, or war ; those of our brethren who suffer persecution for the sake of the Gospel ; all such as are in danger by sea or land, and all persons oppressed with poverty, sickness, or any other distress of body or sorrow of mind. We pray particularly for the sick and afflicted members of this Church, and for all who have desired the aid of our prayers. May it please Thee to show them Thy fatherly kindness, and to deliver them out of all their troubles ; above all, grant them the consolations of which they have need, dispose them to patience and resignation, and make their afflictions promote the salvation of their souls.

4.

FINALLY, O our God and Father, regard with Thy favour this worshipping assembly. Be pleased to give us all that is needful for us, and grant us grace that we may not abuse Thy mercies, but use them with sobriety, charity, and thankfulness. Remove from us the dangers that may threaten us, and deliver us, above all, from sin. Accept our worship, notwithstanding its imperfections, and grant that henceforth, putting all our trust in Thy wellbeloved Son, enlightened by His instructions, guided by His example, and sanctified by His Spirit, we may walk in newness of life, and so prepare for that blessed life which Thou hast promised to Thy children in heaven.

Hear us, O merciful Father, in these our supplications, for the sake of Thy dear Son Jesus Christ, our Lord, to whom, with Thee and the Holy Ghost, be all honour and glory, world without end.*

   Amen.

II.

O LORD our heavenly Father, high and mighty, King of kings, Lord of lords, the only Ruler of princes, who dost from Thy throne behold all the dwellers upon earth: most heartily we beseech Thee with Thy favour to behold her most sacred Majesty Queen Victoria, and so replenish her with the grace of Thy

---

 * The above is a version of the intercession of the Reformed Church, authorised in substance by the Church of Scotland in the 'Book of Common Order.'

Holy Spirit that she may always incline to Thy will, and walk in Thy way; endue her plenteously with heavenly gifts; grant her in health and wealth long to live; strengthen her that she may vanquish and overcome all her enemies; and finally, after this life, she may attain everlasting joy and felicity, through Jesus Christ our Lord.

Almighty God, the fountain of all goodness, we humbly beseech Thee to bless Albert Edward, Prince of Wales, the Princess of Wales, and all the Royal Family. Endue them with Thy Holy Spirit; enrich them with Thy heavenly grace; prosper them with all happiness; and bring them to thine everlasting kingdom, through Jesus Christ our Lord.

[Most gracious God, we humbly beseech Thee, as for this kingdom in general, so especially for the high court of Parliament at this time assembled, that thou wouldest be pleased to direct and prosper all their consultations to the advancement of Thy glory, the good of Thy Church, the safety, honour, and welfare of our sovereign and her dominions; that all things may be so ordered and settled by their endeavours upon the best and surest foundations; that peace and happiness, truth and justice, religion and piety, may be established among us for all generations.]

We beseech Thee to hear us, good Lord:

That it may please Thee to endue the Lords of the Council and all the nobility with grace, wisdom, and understanding:

That it may please Thee to bless and keep the magistrates, giving them grace to execute justice and to maintain truth:

That it may please Thee to bless and keep all the people:

That it may please Thee to give and preserve to our use the kindly fruits of the earth, so as in due time we may enjoy them:

That it may please Thee to give to all nations unity, peace, and concord.

WE beseech Thee to hear us, good Lord: That it may please Thee to rule and govern Thy holy Church universal in the right way:

That it may please Thee to illuminate all pastors and ministers of Thy Church with true knowledge and understanding of Thy Word, and that both by their preaching and living they may set it forth and show it accordingly:

That it may please Thee to remove all false doctrine, heresy, and schism:

That it may please Thee to give to all Thy people increase of grace to hear meekly Thy Word, and to receive it with pure affection, and to bring forth the fruits of the Spirit:

That it may please Thee to bring into the

way of truth all such as have erred and are deceived:

That it may please Thee to strengthen such as do stand, and to comfort and help the weakhearted, and to raise up them that do fall, and finally to beat down Satan under our feet.

WE beseech thee to hear us, good Lord:
That it may please Thee to succour, help, and comfort all who are in danger, necessity, and tribulation:

That it may please Thee to preserve all who travel by land or by water, all women in the perils of childbirth, all sick persons and young children, and to show Thy pity upon all prisoners and captives:

That it may please Thee to defend and provide for the fatherless children and widows, and all who are desolate and oppressed:

That it may please Thee to have mercy upon all men.

O GOD, merciful Father, that despisest not the sighing of a contrite heart, nor the desire of such as be sorrowful, mercifully assist our prayers that we make before Thee in all our troubles and adversities whensoever they oppress us; and graciously hear us, that those evils which the craft and subtilty of the devil or man worketh against us be brought to nought, and by the providence of Thy goodness they may be dispersed, that we Thy servants, being hurt by no persecutions, may evermore give thanks unto Thee in Thy holy Church, through Jesus Christ our Lord.

O God, from whom all holy desires, all good counsel, and all just works do proceed, give unto Thy servants that peace which the world cannot give, that our hearts may be set to obey Thy commandments; and also that we, being defended from the fear of our enemies, may by Thy protection pass our time in peace and quietness; through Jesus Christ our Lord.*

Amen.

III.

1.

ALMIGHTY God, King of kings and Lord of lords, we pray for our sovereign lady Queen Victoria, that Thou wouldst grant her a long and happy life, faithful counsellors, loyal

---

* The English Liturgy (2d Book of Edward VI.) was, by the authority of the Lords of the Congregation, read in the churches of Scotland for some years after the Reformation. The prayer for the Queen given above was retained in the Book of Common Order, and the portions of the Litany are mainly from reformed versions—Bucer's and the German Reformed.

subjects, a prosperous reign, and finally bestow upon her a crown of glory.

We pray for Albert Edward, Prince of Wales, the Princess of Wales, and all the Royal family, that Thou wouldst regard them with Thy favour, and so dispose their hearts that, wherever scattered, they may be nursing-fathers and nursing-mothers to the Church.

We pray for the high court of Parliament, for the nobles, rulers, judges, and magistrates of the land, that Thou wouldst inspire them with Thy wisdom and grant them Thy blessing.

We pray for the army and navy, that they may be distinguished by loyalty and valour, temperance and godliness.

We pray for the empire and all its colonies, beseeching Thee to preserve our peace and defend our liberties, to prosper our trade and commerce, to send healthful and seasonable weather, to bless our husbandry, and to crown the year with Thy goodness.

2.

ALMIGHTY God, who hast made of one blood all nations, we pray for the peace of the whole world and the salvation of all men. Look in pity upon Thine ancient people, whose are the fathers, and of whom according to the flesh Jesus Christ our Lord and Saviour came ;

and have mercy upon all who are in bondage to heathen superstition, and fetch them home, blessed Lord, to Thy flock, that they may be saved among the remnant of the true Israelites.

We pray especially for the good estate of the catholic Church, that the time to favour Sion, yea, the set time, may soon come; that the divisions which desolate Thine heritage may be healed; that what is wanting anywhere may be supplied; and that every plant that is not of Thy planting may be rooted up. O God, we have heard with our ears, and our fathers have told us, the noble works that Thou didst in their days and in the old time before them. O Lord, arise, help us, and deliver us for Thine honour.

We pray for all pastors and ministers of Thy Word, that they may take heed to themselves and to all the flocks over which the Holy Ghost hath made them bishops, to feed the Church of God which He hath purchased with His blood, that when the chief Shepherd shall appear they may receive a crown of glory that fadeth not away.

We pray for this parish, that those among us who bear office may be ensamples to the flock; that the young may abide in Christ, into whom they have been ingrafted, and be spared for lives of piety and usefulness; that the middle-aged may be strong for the Lord and valiant for the right; and that those advanced in years may have bodily comfort and joy in the Holy Ghost, and finally a good end and an abundant entrance into rest.

3.

WE pray for the poor and needy, the desolate and the oppressed, the widow and the orphan, the weak and the bowed-down, beseeching Thee to remember them in mercy and to visit them in Thy compassion.

We pray for those who mourn, that they may be comforted; for those who suffer pain and anguish, that they may be relieved; for those in sickness, that they may be healed, and may again praise Thee in the sanctuary; and especially we commend to Thee the dying, entreating Thee to be with them in that last hour, when heart and flesh do faint and fail, to wash their souls in the blood of Christ, and to receive them into Thy kingdom.

O Thou who art the confidence of the ends of the earth, and of them that are far off upon the sea, we commend to Thy Almighty protection all travellers, sojourners, and strangers. Sail with them who sail, journey with them who journey, and grant to them who are far from their homes that they may revisit them in Thy good time in peace.

O Thou who art the God of all the families of

the earth, we beseech Thee to bless all our friends and kindred, and to grant that we may ever be knit together in the bonds of mutual love, and, above all, that we may be members together of the mystical body of Christ, and so be united by bonds that are eternal. And O God, our heavenly Father, with whom do live the spirits of the just made perfect, we give Thee thanks for all near and dear to us who have been washed from their sins in the blood of the Lamb, and who, having accomplished their warfare, are at rest in the land of the living, amid the delights of Paradise.

4.

FINALLY, O Lord, we pray for each other, all for each, that Thou wouldst bless us outwardly in our bodies, inwardly in our souls, and grant us good success in all our labours. That which is good and profitable do Thou supply unto us. Give us the peace that cometh from above, and also peace in this world. Grant that we may spend the remainder of this day in Thy fear; and may Thy goodness and mercy follow us all our days, and may we dwell in Thy house for evermore.*

Amen.

* The above Intercession is based on the Oriental Liturgies.

IV.

O GOD of infinite mercy, who hast compassion on all men, and relievest the necessities of all that call to Thee for help, hear the prayers of Thy servants who are unworthy to ask anything for themselves, yet in humility and duty are bound to pray for others.*

We pray Thee for all men, as Thou hast taught us, that Thou wouldst bestow upon them all the knowledge of Thy truth.

We pray Thee to deliver the heathen from idolatry, and gather them into Thy holy Church; that, by acknowledging the Light which is Christ, they may be rescued from their own darkness.

We pray Thee for our native lands, and for Thy servant her most sacred Majesty Queen Victoria, that it would please Thee to grant her Thy Holy Spirit, and increase the same from time to time in her, that she may, with a pure faith, acknowledge Jesus Christ, Thine only Son, our Lord, to be King of all kings, and Governor of all governors, even as Thou hast given all power unto Him, both in heaven and on earth, and so give herself wholly to serve Him, and to advance His kingdom in her dominions, that we, being maintained in peace and tranquillity, both here and everywhere, may serve Thee in all

* Jeremy Taylor.

holiness and virtue; and finally being delivered from all fear of enemies, may render thanks unto Thee all the days of our life.*

We pray Thee to bless Albert Edward, Prince of Wales, the Princess of Wales, and all the members of the Royal Family.

We pray for all rulers, judges, and magistrates, that Thou wouldst give the spirit of wisdom to those to whom Thou hast given the authority of government;† and that we, under those set in authority over us, may lead quiet and peaceful lives, in all godliness and honesty.

We pray for Thy holy catholic Church upon earth, that, guided with Thy perpetual governance, she may walk warily in times of quiet, and boldly in times of trouble; that those who love her may abide in her peace, and those who depart from her may one day come back to her communion, and that when all sorrows are taken away, we may be refreshed with the joys of an eternal resurrection.‡

We pray for those who minister in holy things; let Thy power come to the aid of Thy servants, and clothe them with glory and beauty, and so perfect Thy gifts in them that they may carefully discharge their ministry according to Thy pleasure, and at the last may enter into Thine eternal joy.§

* Knox's Liturgy. † Gregorian.
‡ Mosarabic. § Syro-Nestorian Ordinal.

[*Here may be offered prayers for a particular Church, parish, or person.*]

WE pray for those who wander in doubt and uncertainty amid the darkness of this world, and for all who are hardened through the deceitfulness of sin: vouchsafe them grace to come to themselves; the will and the power to return unto Thee, and the loving welcome of Thy forgiveness.

We pray for all in sickness and distress, that Thou wouldst give strength to the weary, aid to the sufferers, comfort to the sad, and help to all in tribulation.*

We pray Thee for the dying, that the souls of Thy servants may be released in peace, and that, dying to the world, they may live to Thee.†

Be present, O Lord, to our prayers, and protect us by day and by night; that in all successive changes of times we may ever be strengthened by Thine unchangeableness, through Jesus Christ our Lord.

Glory be to the Father, and to the Son, and to the Holy Ghost; as it was in the beginning, is now, and ever shall be: world without end.

Amen.

---

* Ambrosian.   † Gregorian.

V.

REMEMBER, O Lord, Thy holy Catholic and Apostolic Church, which is from one end of the earth to the other. Give peace to her whom Thou hast purchased with the precious blood of Thy Christ, and establish Thy holy house to the end of the world.

Remember, O Lord, all who bear rule in Thy Church, who rightly divide the bread of Thy word of truth, and let none of us be confounded who surround Thy holy altar.

Remember, O Lord, those who bring forth fruit, and do good works in Thy Church, and who remember the poor. Recompense them with rich and heavenly gifts. Render to them, instead of earthly things, the heavenly: instead of the temporal, the eternal; instead of corruptible, the incorruptible.

Remember, O Lord, all those whom Thou hast deemed right to make to reign upon the earth, especially Thy servant her most sacred Majesty Queen Victoria, Albert Edward, Prince of Wales, and all the Royal Family. With the helmet of truth, with the crown of Thy good pleasure, endue them, O Lord; exalt their right hand; establish their kingdom. Give them a deep peace that none can take away; and speak in their hearts for the good of Thy Church, and of all Thy people.

Remember, O Lord, the whole body of the people, all those present before Thee, and those who are absent for a reasonable cause; and have compassion upon them, and upon us, according to the multitude of Thy mercies. Fill their stores with every good thing; keep their families in peace and concord; bring up the little ones; teach the young; strengthen the old; comfort the disheartened; gather those who are scattered; bring back those who have gone astray; travel with the travellers by sea or land; take care of the widows; protect the orphans; deliver the captive; heal the sick.

Remember, O Lord, those who are in any tribulation, necessity, or danger; all those who are in need of Thy great compassions; those who love us or hate us; those who have given us charge, unworthy as we are, to pray for them; and those whom we have omitted to mention through ignorance or forgetfulness: do Thou, O Lord, remember them who knowest the state and occupation of every one. Be Thou all to all, who knowest each heart and its request, each house and its need. Keep the righteous in righteousness; make the wicked good through Thy goodness.

Visit us in Thy kindness; manifest Thyself unto us in Thy love. Grant us temperate and favourable seasons; deliver us from fire and pestilence, from famine and sword; appease the discussions of the Churches; repress the tumults of nations; bring to naught the risings of heresies.

Receive us all into Thy kingdom, showing us to be children of the day and of the light; and grant us now, and evermore, Thy peace and Thy love, O Lord our God, for Thou alone hast given, and givest, us all things.*

Glory be to the Father, and to the Son, and to the Holy Ghost; as it was in the beginning, is now, and ever shall be: world without end.

Amen.

VI.

LORD God, our heavenly Father, we beseech Thee to govern by Thy Holy Spirit the Christian Church, with all her ministers and teachers, that she may preserve the pure teaching of Thy Word to the awakening and strengthening of love toward Thee and toward all men.

Let Thy mercy, O Lord, be great toward Thy servant our Sovereign the Queen, the Prince and Princess of Wales, the whole Royal family, and all connected with them. Grant to them

* Liturgy of St Basil, adapted.

long life, that they may be a continual blessing and Christian example to the people ; and grant to all in authority in this land a wise heart, a sound judgment, a courageous spirit, and a strong sense of duty, that we, under their protection, may live quiet and peaceable lives in all godliness and honesty.

Protect the royal army, and all true servants of the Queen and country, that their services may be blessed to Thy honour, and to the good of the people. Bless all Christian lands. Of Thy mercy direct the education and upbringing of the young, that they may grow in Thy fear and to the praise of Thy name. Further every Christian enterprise, and grant unto all men to live honestly, walking before Thee in a good conscience.

Remember for good all in trouble or poverty, all who are forsaken of men, all who are in sickness, or in want, or in any kind of danger. O God of all consolation, keep them strong in faith and patience, and give them deliverance as it seemeth good to Thy fatherly wisdom.

Be the Saviour of all men, especially of Thy faithful ones. Preserve us from the death of the wicked and impenitent. Prepare us more and more for the end of the righteous. Grant, O Lord, that we may live in Thy fear, die in Thy favour, depart hence in peace, rest in the grave under Thy protection, be raised by Thy power, and thereafter inherit the blessed hope of eternal life, for the sake of Thy dear Son, our Lord Jesus Christ.

Glory be to the Father, and to the Son, and to the Holy Ghost; as it was in the beginning, is now, and ever shall be: world without end.*

Amen.

VII.

ALMIGHTY and ever-living God, who by Thy holy Apostle hast taught us to make prayers and supplications, and to give thanks for all men, we humbly beseech Thee most mercifully to receive these our prayers, which we offer unto Thy Divine Majesty, beseeching Thee to inspire continually the universal Church with the spirit of truth, unity, and concord; and grant that all they who do confess Thy holy name may agree in the truth of Thy holy Word, and live in unity and godliness. We beseech Thee also to save and defend all Christian kings, princes, and governors, and especially Thy servant Victoria, our Queen, that under her we may be godly and quietly governed; and grant unto her whole Council, and to all who are put in authority under her, that they may truly and

* Lutheran Liturgy.

indifferently minister justice to the punishment of wickedness and vice, and to the maintenance of Thy true religion and virtue. Give grace, O heavenly Father, to all who bear rule in Thy Church, that they may both, by their life and doctrine, set forth Thy true and lively Word, and rightly and duly administer Thy holy Sacraments; and to all Thy people give Thy heavenly grace, and especially to this congregation now present, that with meek heart and due reverence they may hear and receive Thy Holy Word, truly serving Thee in holiness and righteousness all the days of their life. And we most humbly beseech Thee of Thy goodness, O Lord, to comfort and succour all them who, in this transitory life, are in trouble, sorrow, need, sickness, or any other adversity. And we also bless Thy holy name for all Thy servants departed this life in Thy faith and fear; beseeching Thee to give us grace so to follow their good examples, that with them we may be partakers of Thy heavenly kingdom.

Assist us mercifully, O Lord, in these our supplications and prayers, and dispose the way of Thy servants towards the attainment of everlasting salvation, that amongst all the changes and chances of this mortal life they may ever be defended by Thy most gracious and ready help; through Jesus Christ our Lord.

Glory be to the Father, and to the Son, and to

the Holy Ghost; as it was in the beginning, is now, and ever shall be: world without end.
Amen.

VIII.

O THOU who acceptest the intercessions which Thy servants offer up in Thy Son's name, remember, we beseech Thee, every creature of Thine for good, and visit the whole world with Thy mercy.

O Thou Preserver and Lord of men, think graciously upon mankind; and as Thou hast concluded all under sin and unbelief, so let Thy pity and Thy pardon extend unto all.

O Thou Lord of the harvest, send forth, we pray Thee, labourers fitted in all points to do the work of that harvest. Let the Sun of Righteousness give light to those who sit in darkness. Let Thy gospel have free course and be glorified.*

O Thou great King of all the earth, preserve, we beseech Thee, all Christian princes, more especially her most sacred Majesty Queen Victoria, Albert Edward, Prince of Wales, the Princess of Wales, and all the members of the Royal Family; that, being faithful servants of

* Bishop Andrews.

Thee, the King of kings, they may inherit the crown of everlasting glory.

O Thou who distributest among men degrees of power severally as Thou wilt, grant that all persons of eminence and authority may be eminent for virtue and sincere regard to Thy holy faith. Fill them with all godly wisdom; guide them in the administration of justice to all persons and in all causes; and give all Thy people grace to live in subjection to them, not only for wrath, but also for conscience' sake.

O Thou who art the wholesome defence and strength of Thine Anointed, bless, we beseech Thee, Thy holy catholic Church; remove all her divisions, root out of her all heresies and false doctrines, let her live by Thy Spirit, and reign in Thy glory, bring back to the fold those who have erred and strayed therefrom, and grant that all who confess Thy holy name may agree in the truth of Thy Holy Word, and live in unity and godly concord.

O Thou who art the reward of them that wait upon Thee, send down a double portion of Thy Spirit upon those whom Thou hast set apart to minister in holy things, that they may do it with clean hands and pure hearts, that they may be guides to the blind, comforters to the weary and heavy-laden, that they may strengthen the weak and confirm the strong, that they may boldly rebuke sin, and patiently suffer for the truth.

[*Here may be offered prayers for any particular Church, parish, or person.*]

O THOU Helper of the helpless, our seasonable refuge in the time of trouble, remember all who are under any sort of extremity, and call upon Thee for succour and protection, relieve all their necessities and lighten their burdens, give them patience and submission to Thy blessed will, and in Thy due time deliver them from all their troubles. And especially we commend into Thy merciful hands the souls of Thy servants departing from the body, most humbly beseeching Thee that they may be precious in Thy sight; receive them into the blessed arms of Thine unspeakable mercy, into the sacred rest of everlasting peace, and into the glorious estate of Thy chosen saints in heaven.

Finally, O Lord, we commit to Thy custody and protection now, henceforth, and for ever, our soul and body, our minds and thoughts, our prayers and desires, our life and death, our kindred and friends, our neighbours and acquaintances, those who have asked us to pray for them, and all those for whom we ought of ourselves specially to pray. God the Father preserve and keep us; God the Son assist and strengthen us; God the Holy Ghost defend and aid us; God the Holy Trinity be ever with us. Let Thy merciful kindness be upon us, even as we do put our trust in Thee.

Glory be to the Father, and to the Son, and to the Holy Ghost; as it was in the beginning, is now, and ever shall be: world without end.

Amen.

XI.

Concluding Collects.

I.

O LORD God Almighty, who art always and in all things, who wast before all, and wilt be ever more in all, God blessed for evermore, to Thee we commit, now and for ever, our soul and body, our thoughts, affections, words, and actions, all things that we have without us, and all that we are within, our heart and mind and memory, our faith and life, all we commit into Thy hands, that Thou mayest guard and keep them by day and night, at all hours and at every moment. Hear us, holy Father, and preserve us from all harm and sin, from all snares and assaults of the devil, and from all enemies visible and invisible;* through Jesus Christ our Lord.
Amen.
* Augustine.

II.

WE humbly beseech Thee, O heavenly Father, to do away as the night all our transgressions, and to scatter our sins as the morning cloud: Lord, forgive whatever thou hast seen amiss in us during our past lives. Wash us thoroughly from our iniquity, and cleanse us from our sin; and let Thy Holy Spirit so prevent, and accompany, and follow us during this day and all our days, that we may believe in Thee, love Thee, and keep Thy commandments, and continue in Thy fear all the day long; through Jesus Christ our Lord.*

Amen.

III.

GOD of all power and glory, who hast not appointed us unto wrath, but to obtain salvation by our Lord Jesus Christ, perfect and fulfil in us, we beseech Thee, the work of Thy redeeming mercy, that being delivered more and more from our sins, we may be able to serve Thee in newness of life. Sanctify us in body, soul, and spirit, and guide us evermore in the way of peace. Help us to overcome the world. Beat down Satan under our feet. Give us cour-

* Goulburn.

age to confess Christ always, and patience to endure in His service unto the end, that having finished our course with joy, we may rest in hope, and finally attain to the resurrection of the just, through the infinite merits of our Saviour Jesus Christ.*
>
> Amen.

IV.

O LORD most mighty and most merciful, we commend ourselves unto Thee and to the Word of Thy grace, which is able to build us up and to give us an inheritance among all them that are sanctified. We beseech Thee to keep our souls from death, our eyes from tears, and our feet from falling, that we may walk before Thee in the light of the living, and at the last may be presented faultless before the presence of Thy glory with exceeding joy; through Jesus Christ our Saviour.
>
> Amen.

V.

HASTEN, we entreat Thee, O Lord, the second and glorious appearing of Thy Son, our Saviour Jesus Christ; and grant unto us that, daily looking for that blessed hope, we

---

* German Reformed Church.

may not sleep as do others, but may watch and be sober, exercising ourselves unto godliness, and working out our own salvation with fear and trembling; that we, with all Thy saints, may be presented holy and unblamable before the presence of Thy glory with exceeding joy; through Him that loved us and washed us from our sins in His own blood.

Now to the only wise God, our Saviour, be glory and majesty, dominion and power, both now and ever.
   Amen.

VI.

WE commit ourselves and all that are dear to us, our kindred, friends, and benefactors, and those who have desired to be remembered in our prayers, to Thy mercy and grace, and to the keeping of Thy good providence, O Lord our God.

Grant unto them and us Thy blessing, which maketh rich and addeth no sorrow.

Cleanse our souls with the presence of Thy good and holy Spirit: adorn them with the ornaments of Thy grace: sanctify us wholly in spirit, and soul, and body; and preserve us blameless to the coming and kingdom of our Lord.
  Amen.

XII.

Collects,

Which may be used in the foregoing Services, wherever they are appropriate.

For Purity.

ALMIGHTY God, our most holy and eternal Father, who art of pure eyes, and canst behold no iniquity, let Thy gracious and holy Spirit descend upon Thy servants, that no impure thoughts may pollute that soul which Thou hast sanctified, no impure words pollute that tongue which Thou hast ordained an organ of Thy praise, no impure action rend the veil of that temple which Thou hast chosen for an habitation; but grant that, our senses being sealed up from all vain objects, our hearts entirely possessed with religion, fortified with prudence, watchfulness, and self-denial, we may so live in this present world as not to fail of the glories of the world to come.*

Amen.

* Jeremy Taylor, chiefly.

For those who minister in Holy Things.

O THOU great Shepherd and Bishop of our souls, give unto Thy servants, the ministers of the mysteries of our most holy faith, the spirit of prudence and activity, faith and charity, confidence and zeal, diligence and watchfulness, that they may declare Thy will unto Thy people faithfully, and minister Thy sacraments rightly. Grant, O Lord, that by a holy life and a true belief, by well-doing and patient suffering when Thou dost call them to it, they may glorify Thee, the great lover of souls, and, after a plentiful conversion of sinners from the error of their ways, may shine as the stars in glory.*

Amen.

Against Temptation.

O GOD, who didst suffer Thine own Son to be tempted of the wicked one, that He might be able to succour them that are tempted, we beseech Thee to deliver us from those snares and temptations by which we are continually beset: save us from the evil spirit of guile and deceit; save us from the evil spirit of malice and uncharitableness; save us from the evil spirit of falsehood and uncleanness; and so strengthen us mightily by Thy good Spirit, that in all things we may be more than conquerors through

* Jeremy Taylor, chiefly.

Him that loved us, and washed us from our sins in His own blood.

Amen.

For Guidance.

O THOU great Shepherd of Israel, who, by Thine outstretched arm, didst bring Thy people of old out of the land of Egypt and the house of bondage, guiding them safely through the wilderness to the promised land; we pray Thee to deliver us from the bondage and slavery of our sins, and so to lead us through the wilderness of this world, feeding us with bread from heaven, and with water out of the smitten Rock, and upholding us amid the swellings of Jordan, that we may enter at last into that rest which remaineth for Thy faithful people.

Amen.

Communion of Saints.

ALMIGHTY and everlasting God, who hast enabled Thy saints not only to believe in Thy Son but also to suffer for His sake, extend Thy divine aid to our weakness; that as they breathed out their happy souls for the hope of Thine everlasting mercy, we may at least attain it by a sincere confession of Thee; through Jesus Christ our Lord.*

Amen.

* Leonine (Bright).

Remembrance of the Dead.

BLESSED Lord, with whom do rest the spirits of Thy departed saints, and who hast said unto us by Thy Spirit, "Blessed are the dead who die in the Lord;" enable us to be followers of them, as they were followers of Christ; and so to run our race with patience, and to fight the good fight of faith, that, our course being finished and our warfare accomplished, we may join the innumerable company of Thy redeemed.
    Amen.

The Outer World.

O GOD, who hast made everything beautiful in its season, the glory of whose presence filleth the universe, teach us to see Thee in the works which Thou hast made; that we may worship Thee, who hast so wonderfully and beautifully made them: and inasmuch as the whole creation groaneth and travaileth in pain, being cursed for the sin of man, hasten Thou the kingdom and coming of Thy Christ, who shall restore both it and us in the day of His appearing.
    Amen.

For Grace.

O GOD, with whom it is an easy thing to give life unto the dead, we beseech Thee to increase in our hearts the power of faith which Thou hast given, and to carry onward in us the gifts of Thy grace. Mercifully bestow by Thy Spirit what human frailty cannot attain; that, being severed from thee by no iniquities, we may evermore cleave unto Thee; and as we have known the mystery of Thy life upon earth, we may also perfectly enjoy it in heaven.

Amen.

For Faith.

LET Thy power, O Christ, come to the aid of Thy servants; and so reveal Thyself to our darkened understandings that we may truly believe in Thee; that believing in Thee we may desire Thee; that desiring Thee we may seek Thee; that seeking we may find Thee; that finding we may love Thee; and that loving Thee we may dwell in Thee for ever.*

Amen.

For Perfection in Christ.

O GOD, who art rich in mercy to all, and who madest Thy Son to be the Light

---
* Augustine.

of the world, we beseech Thee to make us complete in Him : give us grace to live as He lived, to suffer with the resignation with which He suffered, and to depart commending our spirits into Thine hands ; that in all things we may be like unto our Elder Brother, the Captain of our salvation, and the Author and Finisher of our faith.
Amen.

For Unity.

O ALMIGHTY God, who didst call out Thy holy Church to be one holy body, filled with Thy divine presence and life, and instructed in Thine eternal truth, have mercy upon all who profess and call themselves Christians ; lead them, we beseech Thee, out of all their wandering and divisions, and heal all mutual hatred, variance, and animosities, that they may all once more be one in Jesus Christ, as He is one with Thee. Deliver all those who are deceived by the wiles of the enemy and have forsaken the congregation of Thy Church, or been carried away by the vanity of error, and restore them to Thy mercy, to the unity of the truth in the one fold of Jesus Christ, Thy holy Church.
Amen.

For Heavenly-mindedness.

O LORD our Maker and Redeemer, the Holy One of Israel, who hast stretched forth the heavens and laid the foundations of the earth, be pleased graciously to confirm and carry forward Thy glorious work of salvation in our hearts, causing old things to pass away and all things to become new; that, looking always above and beyond this world, we may have our conversation in heaven, from whence also we look for the Saviour, the Lord Jesus Christ, who liveth and reigneth with Thee, and the Holy Ghost, ever one God: world without end.*

Amen.

For Heavenly-mindedness.

ALMIGHTY God, the former of our bodies and father of our spirits, in whom we live, move, and have our being, shed abroad Thy love in our hearts, we beseech Thee, and cause the comfort of Thy heavenly grace to abound in us, as the earnest and pledge of joys to come; that, casting away all anxious thought for the transitory things of this world, we may seek first Thy kingdom and righteousness, and labour only for that meat which endureth unto everlasting life; through Jesus Christ our Lord. †

Amen.

* German Reformed.   † Ibid.

For Christian Boldness.

O ALMIGHTY Saviour, who hast taught us by Thine example to bear mocking and evil speaking, grant that we may never be ashamed of Thee and of Thy service; but that the fear of Thee may deliver us from all sinful fear of men, so that we may never be turned aside from doing what is right, either by the violence of the wicked, or through their false enticements; and give us grace manfully to confess Thee before men, that Thou mayest acknowledge us for Thine, when Thou comest to judge the world in righteousness; through Jesus Christ our Lord.
Amen.

For Diligence.

O GOD, who by the example of Thy dear Son hast warned us that we should work Thy works while it is day, before the night cometh, when no man can work, keep us from sloth and idleness, and from the misuse of those talents which Thou hast committed to our trust. Enable us to perform the several duties of our state and calling with such care and diligence that our work may never be reproved in Thy sight; and forasmuch as the needful business of this life is apt to steal away our hearts from Thee, give us grace to remember that we have a Master in heaven, and to do everything in singleness of heart, as unto Thee and not unto men, that of Thee we may receive the reward of the inheritance which Thou hast promised in Thy Son, our Saviour, Jesus Christ.

Amen.

For Diligence.

O GOD, who art the continual defence and protection of all who trust in Thee, and who hast ordained that we should eat bread in the sweat of our brow, we beseech Thee mercifully to prosper the work of our hands, and to sanctify the fruit of our labours to our own good, the good of others, and to Thy glory, and so help us to carry the spirit of Thy holy day into all the business of the week, that whilst our bodies and minds are engaged in honest and useful toil, our hearts may still live and rest in Thee; through Jesus Christ our Lord.

Amen.

For Diligence.

O GOD, who in the beginning didst create the heavens and the earth, and didst give unto all men their work and the bounds of their habitation, grant to us that we be not unwise, but understanding Thy will; not slothful, but diligent in Thy work; that we run not as uncertainly, nor fight Thy battles as those that beat the air; but whatsoever our hand findeth to do, may we do it with our might, that when Thou shalt call Thy labourers to give them their reward, we may so have run that we may obtain, and so have fought the good fight, as to receive the crown of eternal life;* through Jesus Christ our Lord.

Amen.

For Communion with Christ.

O GOD, the Father of our Lord Jesus Christ, of whom the whole family in heaven and earth is named, we beseech Thee, according to the riches of Thy glory, to strengthen us with might by Thy Spirit in the inner man, that Christ may dwell in our hearts by faith; so that being rooted and grounded in love, we may be able to comprehend with all saints what is the breadth, and length, and depth, and height, and to know the love of Christ, which passeth knowledge; to whom, with Thee and the Holy Ghost, be honour and glory: world without end.

Amen.

* Year of Prayer (Alford).

The Glorified Saints.

O GOD, the Father everlasting, whom the glorious hosts of heaven obey, and in whose presence patriarchs, prophets, apostles, martyrs, with all the spirits of the just made perfect, continually do live; fix the eye of our faith, we beseech Thee, with clear and full vision, on the great cloud of witnesses wherewith we are thus compassed about, that laying aside every weight, and the sin that doth so easily beset us, we may run with patience the race that is set before us, and obtain at last the crown of everlasting life; through Jesus Christ our Lord.*

>> Amen.

For Humility.

ALMIGHTY and everlasting God, the Creator of the ends of the earth, who givest power to the faint, and strength to them that have no might, look mercifully, we beseech Thee, on our low estate, and cause Thy grace to triumph in our weakness, that we may arise and follow in the way of righteousness those who by

---

* The Order of Worship for the (American German) Reformed Church.

their faith and patience already inherit the promises; through Jesus Christ our Lord.*

Amen.

For Life in Christ.

WE approach Thee, O God, in the name of Thy holy child Jesus, who, after He had borne our sins and carried our sorrows upon earth, sat down at Thine own right hand, the Mediator of those for whom He died. Grant us, we beseech Thee, to be made partakers, both in that atonement which He perfected on the cross, and in His mediation in the upper sanctuary, that being reconciled through the death of Thy Son, we may be saved by His life, who liveth and was dead, and is alive for evermore, and hath the keys of hell and of death; to whom be glory, both now and for ever.

Amen.

For Spiritual Aid.

O GOD, true and highest Life, by whom, through whom, and in whom, all things live, which live truly and blessedly, pity and help us, according as Thou knowest we need in body and in soul, that being free from the chains

---

* The Order of Worship for the (American German) Reformed Church.

with which we are bound, and casting off all that entangles us, we may serve Thee alone, cleave to Thee alone, and direct every effort towards Thee alone, who knowest all things, and canst perform all things, and who livest for evermore.*

           Amen.

For Holy Intentions.

O ETERNAL God, who hast made all things for man, and man for Thy glory, sanctify our body and soul, our thoughts and intentions, our words and actions, that all we think or speak or do may by us be designed to the glorification of Thy name. Let no pride or self-seeking, no covetousness or revenge, no little ends or low imaginations, pollute our spirit and unhallow any of our words and actions, but let our body be the servant of our spirit, and both body and spirit servants of Jesus, that doing all things for Thy glory here, we may be partakers of Thy glory hereafter; through Jesus Christ our Lord.†

  Amen.

For Various Graces.

O THOU gracious Father of mercy, Father of our Lord Jesus Christ, have mercy upon Thy servants who bow before Thee; par-

---

* Augustine.   † Jeremy Taylor.

don and forgive us all our sins; give us the grace of true repentance, and a strict obedience to Thy holy Word; strengthen us in the inner man for all the parts and duties of our calling and holy living; preserve us for ever in the unity of Thy holy Church, in the integrity of the Christian faith, in the love of God and of our neighbours, and in the hope of life eternal.*
          Amen.

For Restoration.

O GOD, who art long-suffering and kind, and art evermore seeking to turn us from our vanities that we may live and not die, grant that we may know this the time of our visitation, and give ear to the voice that calleth us, and so bring us home, good Lord, from wandering in the wilderness, and give our weary hearts such rest in Thee that we may seek to wander from Thee no more, but abide in Thy peace for ever.
 Amen.

For Divine Knowledge.

MOST gracious God, whom to know is the very bliss and felicity of man's soul, and yet none can know Thee unless Thou wilt

* Jeremy Taylor.

open and show Thyself unto him, vouchsafe of Thine infinite mercy now and ever to enlighten our hearts and minds to know Thee and Thy most perfect and holy will, to the honour and glory of Thy name.*

    Amen.

For a Sense of our Mortality.

O GOD, whose days are without end and whose mercies cannot be numbered, make us, we beseech Thee, deeply sensible of the shortness and uncertainty of human life; and let Thy Holy Spirit lead us through this vale of misery in righteousness and holiness all the days of our lives; that when we shall have served Thee in our generation, should it please Thee that we depart hence before the coming of the Lord, we may be gathered to our fathers, having the testimony of a good conscience, in the communion of the Christian Church, in the confidence of a certain faith, in the comfort of a reasonable, religious, and holy hope, in favour with Thee our God, and in perfect charity with all men.†

    Amen.

   * Leighton.   † Jeremy Taylor.

For Love.

CONFIRM, O Lord, we pray Thee, the hearts of Thy children, and strengthen them with the power of Thy grace, that they may both be devout in prayer to Thee and sincere in love for each other; through Jesus Christ our Lord.*

Amen.

For Knowledge.

O THOU who art Light, and in whom is no darkness at all, shine into our darkened hearts, we beseech Thee, dispelling every vain and unholy imagination, making clear to us at all times the way in which we should walk, and guiding us at length into the heavenly city, where there shall be no night any more for ever; through Jesus Christ our Lord.

Amen.

For Temperance.

ALMIGHTY God, gracious Father of men and angels, who openest Thine hand and fillest all things with plenty, teach us to use the gifts of Thy providence soberly and temperately,

* Leonine.

that our temptations may not be too strong for us, our bodies healthless, or our affections sensual and unholy: grant, O Lord, that the blessings which Thou givest us may neither minister to sin nor to sickness, but to health and holiness and thanksgiving; that in the strength of Thy provisions we may faithfully and diligently serve Thee, may worthily feast at Thy table here, and be accounted worthy to sit down at Thy table hereafter; through Jesus Christ our Lord.*

Amen.

For Fellowship with Christ.

BLESSED Lord, who didst choose our sadness and sorrows, that we might be made partakers of Thy glories, let Thine hands support us, Thine eyes pity us, Thy feet tread down every difficulty in our way to heaven: may we dwell in Thy heart, choose with Thy will, and be clothed with Thy righteousness; that in the day of judgment we may be found having on Thy garments, and sealed with Thy impression; and that, bearing on every faculty and member the character of our Elder Brother, we may not be cast out with strangers or unbelievers.†

Amen.

---

* Jeremy Taylor, chiefly.   † Ibid.

COLLECTS.

For Peace.

O GOD, from whom all holy desires, all good counsels, and all just works do proceed, give unto Thy servants that peace which the world cannot give; that both our hearts may be set to obey Thy commandments, and also that by Thee, we, being defended from the fear of our enemies, may pass our time in rest and quietness; through the merits of Jesus Christ our Saviour.*
   Amen.

For Heavenly Aid.

O GOD, the protector of them that trust in Thee, without whom nothing is strong, nothing is holy, increase and multiply upon us Thy mercy, that Thou being our Ruler and Guide, we may so pass through things temporal that we finally lose not the things eternal; grant this, O heavenly Father, for Jesus Christ's sake.†
   Amen.

For the Church.

GRACIOUS Father, we humbly beseech Thee for Thy holy catholic Church: fill it with all truth; in all truth with all peace;

 * Anglican.   † Ibid.

when it is corrupt, purge it; when it is in error, reform it; when it is superstitious, rectify it; when it is right, strengthen and confirm it; when it is in want, furnish it; when it is divided and rent asunder, make up the breaches of it, O Thou Holy One of Israel.*

Amen.

For Preparation for the Coming of Christ.

ALMIGHTY God, we beseech Thee grant unto Thy people grace that they may wait with vigilance for the advent of Thy Son our Lord, that when He shall arise from Thy right hand to visit the earth in righteousness and Thy people with salvation, He may not find us sleeping in sin, but diligent in Thy service, and rejoicing in Thy praises, that so we may enter in with Him unto the marriage of the Lamb; through His merits, who liveth and reigneth with Thee and the Holy Ghost, ever one God: world without end.

Amen.

Advent of Christ.

GOD of all grace and comfort, who hast not appointed us unto wrath, but to obtain salvation by our Lord Jesus Christ, aid us, we

---

* Archbishop Laud's Devotions.

beseech Thee, at this time, to repent heartily and truly of all our sins, and so to humble ourselves that when He cometh we may be prepared to receive Him with childlike faith, and join in the glad cry, Hosanna to the Son of David! Blessed is He that cometh in the name of the Lord!*

Amen.

Advent of Christ.

CLEANSE our conscience, we beseech Thee, Almighty God, by the daily visitation of Thy grace, that when Thy Son and our Lord, Jesus Christ, shall come, He may find us fit for His appearing, and ready to meet Him without spot in the company of all His saints; who liveth and reigneth with Thee and the Holy Ghost, ever one God: world without end.†

Amen.

Advent of Christ.

INCLINE, O Lord, we beseech Thee, Thine ear to our prayers, and visit the darkness of our mind with the dayspring from on high; that at the second coming of Thy Son to judge the world, we may hasten with joy to meet Him, who liveth and reigneth with Thee and

---

* The Order of Worship for the (American German) Reformed Church.   † Ibid.

the Holy Ghost, ever one God: world without end.*
Amen.

The Incarnation of our Lord.

MOST merciful God, who hast so loved the world as to give Thine only-begotten Son, that whosoever believeth in Him should not perish but have everlasting life; vouchsafe unto us, we humbly pray Thee, the precious gift of faith, whereby we may know that the Son of God is come; and, being always rooted and grounded in the mystery of the Word made flesh, may have power to overcome the world, and gain the blessed immortality of heaven; through the merits of this same incarnate Christ, who liveth and reigneth with Thee in the unity of the Holy Ghost, ever one God: world without end.†
Amen.

Manifestation of Christ.

O GOD, the fountain of all truth and grace, who hath called us out of darkness into marvellous light by the glorious gospel of Thy Son, grant unto us power, we beseech Thee, to walk worthy of this vocation, with all lowliness and meekness, endeavouring to keep the unity

---

* The Order of Worship for the (American German) Reformed Church. † Ibid.

of the spirit in the bond of peace; that we may have our fruit unto holiness, and the end everlasting life; through Jesus Christ our Lord.*
Amen.

The Passion and Death of Christ.

O MOST merciful Father, who of Thy tender compassion towards us guilty sinners didst give Thine only-begotten Son to be an offering for our sins, grant us grace, we humbly beseech Thee, that, being united unto Him by Thy Spirit, and made partakers of His sufferings and His death, we may crucify the corrupt inclinations of the flesh, die daily unto the world, and lead holy and unblamable lives. Cleaving unto His cross in all the temptations of life, may we hold fast the profession of our faith without wavering, and finally attain unto the resurrection of the just; through the merits of this same once crucified, but now risen and exalted Saviour.
Amen.

The Passion and Death of Christ.

LORD Jesus Christ, Thou holy and spotless Lamb of God, who didst take upon Thyself the curse of sin which was due to us, with

* The Order of Worship for the (American German) Reformed Church.

all the heavenly host of the redeemed, we unite in ascribing unto Thee power, and riches, and wisdom, and strength, and honour, and glory, and blessing. We bless Thee for all the burdens Thou hast borne, for all the tears Thou hast wept, for all the pains Thou hast suffered, for every drop of blood Thou hast shed, for every word of comfort Thou hast spoken on the cross, for every conflict with the powers of darkness, and for Thine eternal victory over the terrors of death and the pains of hell.*

Amen.

The Resurrection of Christ.

ALMIGHTY God, who hast brought again from the dead our Lord Jesus, the glorious Prince of salvation, with everlasting victory over hell and the grave; grant unto us power, we beseech Thee, to rise with Him to newness of life, that we may overcome the world with the victory of faith, and have part at last in the resurrection of the just; through the merits of the same risen Saviour, who liveth and reigneth with Thee and the Holy Ghost, ever one God: world without end.†

Amen.

*. The Order of Worship for the (American German) Reformed Church.   † Ibid.

COLLECTS. 141

The Descent of the Holy Spirit.

GOD of all peace and consolation, who didst gloriously fulfil the great promise of the Gospel by sending down Thy Holy Ghost on the day of Pentecost to establish the Church as the house of His continual presence and power among men, mercifully grant unto us, we beseech Thee, this same gift of the Spirit to renew, illuminate, refresh, and sanctify our dying souls, to be over us and around us like the light and dew of heaven, and to be in us evermore as a well of water springing up into everlasting life: through Jesus Christ our Lord; to whom, with Thee and the Holy Ghost, ever one God, be honour and glory: world without end.

Amen.

For the Season of Holy Communion.

O GOD, Father of our Lord Jesus Christ, who dost, in Thy good providence, call us to draw near to Thee in Holy Communion, look graciously, we beseech Thee, upon Thy servants who are about to seek Thy grace in this most sacred ordinance. Give unto them true and hearty sorrow for past sins, power to

confess the same unto Thee, grace to seek Thy mercy and forgiveness, and an earnest desire to walk before Thee in newness and holiness of life; and mercifully grant that we, with all those who shall come to Thy holy Table, may be filled with Thy Spirit in the inner man; that drawing near with penitent hearts and lively faith, we may receive the Holy Sacrament to our present and everlasting comfort; through Thy Son our Saviour, Jesus Christ.
Amen.

At the Beginning of the Year.

ALMIGHTY and eternal God, with whom one day is as a thousand years, and a thousand years as one day, we bring Thee thanks and praise for Thy blessings, more than we can number, with which Thou hast crowned our lives during the year now past; and, since Thy mercies are ever new, let the year which has now begun be to us a year of grace and salvation. Have pity upon us in our misery, whose days are as the grass; deliver us from the vanity of our fallen nature, and establish us in the fellowship of that life which is the same yesterday, and to-day, and for ever; graciously protect and conduct us through the uncertainties of this new year of our earthly pilgrimage; pre-

pare us for its duties and trials, its joys and sorrows; help us to watch and pray, and to be always ready like men that wait for their Lord; and grant that every change, whether it be of prosperity or adversity, of life or death, may bring us nearer to Thee, and to that great eternal year of joy and rest, which, after the years of this vain earthly life, awaits the faithful in Thy blissful presence; when we shall unite with angels and saints, in ascribing blessing, and honour, and glory, and power, unto Him who sitteth upon the throne, and unto the Lamb for ever and ever.
  Amen.

Thanksgiving for Harvest.

ALMIGHTY and everlasting God, we yield Thee thanks for Thy bounty again bestowed upon us, who through thy providence and tender mercy have now reaped the fruits of the earth and gathered them into our garners. Give us power to use the same to Thy glory, to the relief of those that are needy, and to our own comfort. Continue, we beseech Thee, Thy loving-kindness unto us, that year by year our land may yield her increase, filling our hearts with food and gladness; and so dispose us by Thy special grace that we Thy servants may never sow only to the flesh, lest of the flesh we reap corruption, but may sow spiritually to life everlasting, and reap the same in thy heavenly kingdom; through Jesus Christ our Lord.*

Amen.

For the Opening of a Church Court.

ALMIGHTY and everlasting God, who by Thy Holy Spirit didst preside in the first synod of the Apostles and Presbyters at Jerusalem, and hast promised to be with Thy Church alway even unto the end of the world, vouchsafe, we pray Thee, unto us Thy servants here assembled Thy gracious presence and benediction. Deliver us from all error, pride, and prejudice. Enlighten us with wisdom from above. Fill our hearts with the spirit of unity and peace; and so order and govern us in all our doings that the kingdom of Satan may be broken down, Thy people comforted and established in their most holy faith, and the pure Gospel truly preached and followed; until at last all Thy dispersed sheep shall be gathered into the one fold of the great Shepherd, Jesus Christ our Lord; to whom be glory for ever and ever.†

Amen.

---

* Order of Worship, German Reformed.   † Ibid.

At Morning Prayer.

O GOD, who dividest the day from the night, separate our deeds from the gloom of darkness. As Thou hast awakened our bodies from sleep, so, we beseech Thee, awaken our souls from sin. As Thou hast caused the light of day to shine on our bodily eyes, cause the light of Thy Word and Holy Spirit to illuminate our heart; and so give us grace, as the children of light, to walk in all holy obedience before Thy face this day, that in all our thoughts, words, and dealings we may endeavour to keep faith and a clean conscience towards Thee and towards all men; through Jesus Christ our Lord.
Amen.

At Morning Prayer.

O LORD our heavenly Father, almighty and everlasting God, who hast safely brought us to the beginning of this day; defend us in the same with Thy mighty power, and grant that this day we fall into no sin, neither run into any kind of danger, but that all our doings may be ordered by Thy governance to do always that which is righteous in Thy sight; through Jesus Christ our Lord.*
Amen.

* Anglican.

At Morning Prayer.

WE give Thee thanks, holy Lord, Father Almighty, everlasting God, who hast been pleased to bring us through the night to the hours of morning; we pray Thee to grant us to pass this day without sin, so that at eventide we may again give thanks to Thee; through Jesus Christ our Lord.*

𝔄men.

At Evening Prayer.

THINE is the day, O Lord, and Thine is the night; grant that the Sun of Righteousness may remain in our hearts to drive away the darkness of wicked thoughts; through Jesus Christ our Lord.

𝔄men.

At Evening Prayer.

ALMIGHTY and everlasting God, at evening and morning and noonday we humbly beseech Thy Majesty that Thou wouldst drive from our hearts the darkness of sins, and make us to come to the true Light, which is Christ, our blessed Lord.

𝔄men.

* Gelasian.

At Evening Prayer.

O LORD God, the Life of mortals, the Light of the faithful, the Strength of those who labour, and the Repose of the blessed dead, grant us a peaceful night free from all disturbance, that after an interval of quiet sleep we may by Thy bounty, at the return of light, be endued with activity by Thy Holy Spirit, and enabled in security to render thanks to Thee.
𝔄men.

XIII.

Canticles,

Which are suitable for public worship, in place of, or along with, the ordinary Psalms, Paraphrases, and Hymns.

Isaiah xii.

Luke i. 46-55.

Luke i. 68-79.

Luke ii. 29-32.

The Te Deum—*We praise Thee*, &c.

XIV.

Benedictions,

Wherewith the whole service may be concluded.

THE Lord bless you and keep you: the Lord cause His face to shine upon you, and be gracious unto you: the Lord lift up His countenance upon you, and give you peace.

Amen.

NOW the God of peace, that brought again from the dead our Lord Jesus, that great Shepherd of the sheep, through the blood of the everlasting covenant, make you perfect in every good work to do His will, working in you that which is well pleasing in His sight, through Jesus Christ; to whom be glory for ever and ever.

Amen.

THE grace of the Lord Jesus Christ, and the love of God, and the communion of the Holy Ghost, be with you all.

     Amen.

THE peace of God, which passeth all understanding, keep your hearts and minds in the knowledge and love of God, and of His Son Jesus Christ our Lord; and the blessing of God Almighty, the Father, the Son, and the Holy Ghost, be amongst you, and remain with you always.

 Amen.

GRACE, mercy, and peace, from God the Father, the Son, and the Holy Ghost, be with you, and with all the people of God, henceforth and for ever.

    Amen.

XV.

THE following Prayers are arranged in the order recommended by the Society, and are here offered as specimens of complete services for the morning and evening of a Lord's Day.

The first set is derived chiefly from the writings of Jeremy Taylor; the second from the prayers in use in the "Holy Catholic Apostolic Church."

FIRST MORNING SERVICE.

Opening Prayer.

I.

FROM the rising of the sun unto the going down of the same the Lord's name is to be praised. The Lord is high above all nations, and His glory above the heavens. Who is like unto the Lord our God, who dwelleth on high, who humbleth Himself to behold the things that are in heaven, and in the earth?

The hour cometh, and now is, when the true worshippers shall worship the Father in spirit and in truth: for the Father seeketh such to worship Him. God is a Spirit: and they that worship Him must worship Him in spirit and in truth.

2.

O ALMIGHTY Father, who dwellest in the light to which no man can approach, in whose presence there is no night, in the light of whose countenance there is perpetual day; we, Thy servants, whom Thou hast preserved during the past night, desire to bless and glorify Thee this morning; and we humbly pray that this day, and all the days of our lives, may be holy and peaceable, healthful to our bodies, and profitable to our souls.

3.

O GOD, the Father of mercies, the Father of our Lord Jesus Christ, have mercy upon Thy servants, and hear the prayers of us miserable sinners.

As for us, we are not worthy to be called Thy children; for we by nature are the vilest of sinners, and the worst of men; lovers of the things of the world, and despisers of the things that are good; greedy of sin, and impatient of reproof; desirous to seem holy, and negligent of being so; full of envy and malice, anger and revenge; earnest in the pursuit of earthly vanities, and slow and soon weary in the things of God and of religion.

O most gracious Lord, enter not into judgment with Thy servants, lest we be consumed in Thy wrath and just displeasure.

4.

O ALMIGHTY God, Thou great Judge of all the world, the Father of our Lord Jesus Christ, the Father of mercies, the Father of men and angels, who desirest not that sinners should perish, but delightest in their conversion and salvation, and hast in our Lord Jesus Christ established the covenant of repentance, and through Him promised pardon to all them that confess their sins and forsake them, be pleased to pardon and forgive all our sins, known and unknown; establish us in Thy perpetual peace; and for ever preserve Thy servants from sinning against Thee, and from suffering Thine eternal anger; for Thy glorious Name's sake.

Hear our prayer, O Lord, and consider our desire: hide not Thy face far from us; put not Thy servants away in anger. Pour out upon us the gift of the Holy Ghost. Give unto us the spirit of prayer, an unreprovable faith, a just and humble hope, and a never-failing charity; a disposition of true humility, a meek and quiet spirit, pure and holy thoughts, clear understanding in the way of godliness, and a holy and edifying conversation. Grant unto us to deny ourselves, to bear the burden of others, to be slow to anger, to fight manfully the battles of the Lord against the flesh, the world, and the devil, to redeem the time, and to walk always as in Thy presence. Impart unto us spiritual wisdom, that we may discern what is pleasing to Thee, and follow what belongs to our peace; let the knowledge and love of Thee and of Jesus Christ our Lord be our guide and our portion all our days; sanctify our souls and bodies here, and glorify them hereafter.

5.

OUR Father which art in heaven, &c.

Prayer after Lessons.

1.

O THOU who art the Father of mercies and the Fountain of life and blessing, we adore and praise and glorify Thy holy name, and give Thee thanks for all the benefits Thou hast conferred upon us. Thou, O God, hast formed us of nothing, and given us a place and being next to the angels, imprinting Thine image upon us, enduing us with reasonable faculties of will and understanding, and giving us a capacity of a blessed immortality. Thou hast caused us to be born in a Christian land, to be baptised with a holy baptism, and to be blessed with a Christian education. Thou hast preserved us by Thy providence and by the ministry of angels from the sword and pestilence, and from every evil accident ; Thou hast fed and clothed us ; Thou hast raised up friends and made them a blessing to us ; Thou hast been our guide in all the paths of life, our hope and confidence in all our griefs and desolations. But above all, Thou hast loved us and all mankind when we were lost and dead, and rebels against Thy divine Majesty ; Thou hast given Thine only-begotten Son to seek and save us. Lord, what is man that Thou art mindful of him, and the son of man that Thou so regardest him? We bless Thee for His love and condescension, for His immaculate holiness, for His holy precepts, for His divine example, for His bitter passion and His death upon the cross, for His triumph over death and hell, for His glorious resurrection and ascension, for His intercession and rule at Thy right hand. We thank thee for the giving of the Holy Ghost, for the Church which Thou hast planted among us, for its ministries and means of grace, for the promises and precepts of Thy Holy Word, and for all the helps and comforts of true religion. Help us with our whole soul evermore to praise Thee, and to live worthy of these Thy benefits.

2.

O LORD God, who givest to men the blessed hope of eternal life by our Lord Jesus Christ, and hast promised Thy Holy Spirit to them that ask Him, be present with us, and with all Thy ministers and people, in the dispensation of Thy Holy Word; grant that we, being preserved from all evil by Thy power, and from all error and false doctrine by the guidance of Thy Holy Spirit, may for ever follow our heavenly calling; that we may not only be hearers of the word of life, but doers also of good works, living a holy and unblameable life in all godliness and honesty before God and the world; that at the end of our mortal life we may enter into the light and life of God, to sing hymns of eternal praise to the glory of Thy name throughout all ages; through Jesus Christ our Lord.

Amen.

Prayer after Sermon.

1.

ALMIGHTY God, our Lord and Master, the Father of mercy and the God of all comfort, we humbly present to Thee the sacrifice of a thankful spirit in a joyful acknowledgment of Thine infinite goodness in sending to us the dayspring from on high to enlighten our darkness and guide our feet into the way of peace. We praise Thy name for that portion of Thy Holy Word of which Thou hast made us partakers this day. Grant that it may bring forth fruit unto Thee and unto holiness in our whole life, to the glory of Thy holy name, the edification of our brethren, and the eternal comfort of our souls in the day of our Lord Jesus.

2.

O GOD of infinite mercy, who hast compassion on all men, and relievest the necessities of all that call to Thee for help, hear the prayers of Thy servants, who are unworthy to ask any petitions for themselves, yet in humility and duty are bound to pray for others.

In mercy remember the Queen; preserve her person in health and honour, her crown in wealth and dignity, her kingdom in peace and plenty, the churches under her protection in piety and knowledge, and a strict and holy religion: keep her perpetually in Thy fear and favour, and crown her with glory and immortality.

O let Thy mercy descend upon the whole Church; preserve her in truth and peace, in unity and safety, in all storms, and against all temptations and enemies; that she, offering to Thy glory the never-ceasing sacrifice of prayer and thanksgiving, may advance the honour of her Lord, and be filled with His Spirit, and partake of His glory.

Remember them that minister about holy things; let Thy priests be clothed with righteousness, and let Thy saints shout for joy.

Be pleased, O Lord, to remember our friends and benefactors; do Thou good to them, and return all their kindness double into their own bosom, rewarding them with blessings, sanctifying them with Thy grace, and bringing them to glory.

Let all our families and kindred, our neighbours and acquaintances, receive the benefit of our prayers and the blessing of the Most High, the comforts and the supports of Thy providence, and the sanctification of Thy Spirit.

Relieve and comfort all the persecuted and afflicted; speak peace to troubled consciences; strengthen the weak; confirm the strong; instruct the ignorant; deliver the oppressed from him that spoileth him, and relieve the needy, and him that hath no helper; and bring us all, by the waters of comfort and in the ways of righteousness, to the kingdom of rest and glory; through Jesus Christ our Lord.

Glory be unto the Father, &c.

THE BENEDICTION.

THE grace of our Lord Jesus Christ, &c.

FIRST EVENING SERVICE.

OPENING PRAYER.

I.

OUR help cometh from the Lord, which made heaven and earth. He will not suffer Thy feet to be moved: He that keepeth Thee will not slumber. Behold, He that keepeth Israel shall neither slumber nor sleep.

God hath not appointed us to wrath, but to obtain salvation by our Lord Jesus Christ, who died for us, that, whether we wake or sleep, we should live together with Him.

2.

O ETERNAL God, Father of men and angels, who hast established the heavens and the earth in a wonderful order, making day and night to succeed each other; we make our humble address to Thy divine Majesty, begging of Thee mercy and protection this night and for ever.

O Lord, pardon all our sins, our light and rash words, the vanity and impiety of our thoughts, our unjust and uncharitable actions, and whatsoever we have transgressed against Thee this day, or at any time before.

3.

ALMIGHTY God, we miserable sinners do humbly confess, and are truly sorrowful, for our many and great, innumerable and intolerable, offences, of which our consciences do accuse us by night and by day, and by which we have provoked Thy severest wrath and indignation against us. We have broken all Thy righteous laws and commandments, by word or by deed, by vain thoughts or sinful desires: we have sinned against Thee in all our relations and capacities, in all places, and at all times; we can neither reckon their number, nor bear their burden, nor suffer Thine anger, which we have deserved. But Thou, O Lord God, art merciful and gracious; have mercy upon us; pardon us for all the evils we have done; judge us not for all the good we have omitted; take not Thy favour from us, but delight Thou to sanctify and save us, and work in us to will and to do of Thy good pleasure all our duty, that, being sanctified by Thy Spirit, and delivered from our sins, we may serve Thee in a religious and holy conversation; through Jesus Christ our Lord.

4

ALMIGHTY God, and most merciful Father, who delightest not in the death of a sinner, but that he be converted from his sin, and Thou be turned from Thine anger; give unto Thy servants a deep contrition for their sins, a perfect hatred, and a full remission, of them; visit us with the joys of Thy salvation, and the sweet sense that Thine anger is turned away from us; grant unto us grace to fear and love Thee, power and will to serve Thee, and time and space to finish the work which Thou hast given us to do; that the souls of Thy servants, being washed in the blood of Jesus, may be justified by Thy mercy, sanctified by Thy Spirit, blessed by Thy providence, and saved by

Thine infinite and eternal goodness; through Jesus Christ our Lord.

Almighty God, the fountain of holiness and of felicity, who, by Thy Word and Spirit, dost conduct all Thy servants in the ways of peace and sanctity, inviting them by Thy promises, winning them by Thy long-suffering, and endearing them by Thy loving-kindness; grant unto us so truly to repent us of our sins, so carefully to reform our errors, so diligently to watch over all our actions, so industriously to perform all our duty, that we may never willingly transgress Thy holy laws: but that it may be the work of our lives to obey Thee, the joy of our souls to please Thee, the satisfaction of all our hopes and the perfection of all our desires to live with Thee in the holiness of Thy kingdom of grace and glory; through Jesus Christ our Lord.

5.

OUR Father which art in heaven, &c.
Amen.

Prayer after Lessons.

I.

SING unto the Lord, O ye saints of His, and give thanks at the remembrance of His holiness ; for His anger endureth but a moment ; in His favour is life : weeping may endure for a night, but joy cometh in the morning.

Thou, Lord, hast preserved us this day, and all our lives, from sin and sorrow, from the violence of the spirits of darkness, from all sad casualties and evil accidents, from the wrath which we have every day deserved.

Thou hast brought up our soul from the grave; Thou hast kept us alive, that we should not go down to the pit. Thou hast showed us marvellous loving-kindness. O Lord our God, we will give thanks unto Thee for ever.

O Lord God of Hosts, who is a strong Lord like unto Thee ? or to Thy faithfulness round about Thee?

Among the gods there is none like unto Thee, O Lord, neither are there any works like unto Thy works. All nations whom Thou hast made shall come and worship before Thee, O Lord, and shall glorify Thy name. For Thou art great, and doest wondrous things. Thou art God alone.

O holy and almighty God, Father of mercies, Father of our Lord Jesus Christ, we adore and praise and glorify Thine infinite and unspeakable love and wisdom, who hast sent Thy Son from Thy bosom to take upon Him our nature, our misery, and our guilt; and hast made the Son of God to become man that we might become the sons of God, and partakers of the Divine nature. We adore Him who did choose our sadness and sorrows, that He might make us partakers of His felicities. We pray that we may dwell in Him in very deed, be instructed with His wisdom, moved by His love, governed by His will, and clothed with His righteousness; that in the day of judgment we may be found to wear His image and likeness, and that, bearing upon every faculty and member the character of our elder Brother, we may not be cast out with strangers and unbelievers.

2.

O GREAT King of heaven and earth, accept and receive Thy servants approaching to the throne of grace with these our prayers and thanksgivings in the name of Jesus Christ; give unto every one of us what is best for us; cast out

all evil from within us; work in us a fulness of holiness, of wisdom, and spiritual understanding, that we, increasing in the knowledge of God, may be fruitful in every good work; through Jesus Christ our Lord.
    Amen.

PRAYER AFTER SERMON.

I.

O ALMIGHTY God, who hast begotten us by Thy Word, renewed us by Thy Spirit, fed us by Thy sacraments, and by the ministry of Thy Church, still go on to build us up to life eternal. Give us understanding in Thy law, that we may know Thy will, and grace and strength faithfully to fulfil the same. Grant that our understandings may know Thee, our hearts may love Thee, and all our faculties and powers give Thee due obedience and service; so that, escaping from the darkness of this world, we may at length come to the land of everlasting rest, in Thy light to behold light and glory; through Jesus Christ our Lord.

2.

O BLESSED God, in mercy remember Thine inheritance, and forget not the congregation of the poor for ever. Preserve the catholic Church in holiness and truth, in unity and peace; give her patience and perseverance in the faith, and do Thou enlarge her borders to the uttermost ends of the earth, that all nations being made partakers of the blessings of the Gospel, Thy name may be glorified, the honour of the Lord Jesus advanced, His prophecies fulfilled, and His coming hastened.

Give the spirit of government and holiness to all Christian kings, princes, and rulers; and do Thou especially show Thy mercy to her most sacred majesty Queen VICTORIA; unite her unto Thee in the bonds of faith and love, preserve her to her life's end in Thy favour, and make her an instrument of glory to Thy name, of blessing to Thy Church, of joy to all faithful people in this kingdom, and crown her with an eternal weight of glory; through Jesus Christ our Lord.

O God, who art rich in mercy, be favourable to ALBERT EDWARD, Prince of Wales, the Princess of Wales, and all the Royal Family, her Majesty's ministers, the Lords and Commons, the magistrates and judges, and all estates of men in this land; give them grace in their several callings to glorify Thee, and to have a conscience void of offence both toward God and toward man, that they may find eternal comfort in the day of the Lord Jesus.

In mercy remember the poor and needy, the widows and the fatherless, the strangers and the friendless, the sick and the dying ; relieve their needs, comfort their sorrows, sanctify their suffering, strengthen their weakness, and in due time deliver them from their sad bondage into the glorious liberty of the sons of God.

Visit, we beseech Thee, O Lord, our habitations with Thy mercy, and us Thy servants with salvation. Let Thy holy angels watch over us, and let the Spirit of the Father illumine our souls. Let no deed of darkness overtake us, and let Thy blessing abide on us for ever ; through Jesus Christ our Lord.

Glory be unto the Father, &c.

Amen.

The Benediction.

THE grace of our Lord Jesus Christ, &c.

Amen.

SECOND MORNING SERVICE.

Opening Prayer.

1.

O COME, let us worship and bow down: let us kneel before the Lord our Maker.

For He is our God; and we are the people of His pasture, and the sheep of His hand.

Be careful for nothing; but in everything, by prayer and supplication with thanksgiving, let your requests be made known unto God.

And the peace of God, which passeth all understanding, shall keep your hearts and minds, through Christ Jesus.

2.

O LORD God, holy and incomprehensible, who didst command light to shine out of darkness, who hast given us rest in sleep, and hast raised us up to glorify and to declare Thy goodness, we beseech Thee of Thy great mercy to accept us who now worship before Thee, and according to our power do give Thee thanks, and to grant unto us our requests for all things pertaining to our everlasting salvation. Make us children of the light and of the day, and heirs of Thine eternal blessing.

From the night early awaketh our soul unto Thee, O God, for the light of Thy commandments is upon the earth. Teach us, O God, by Thy truth, by Thy commandments, by Thy judgments; enlighten the eyes of our minds, lest we sleep the sleep of death. Remove from our hearts all darkness; give unto us the light of the Sun of Righteousness, and preserve our life free from all snares by the aid of Thy Holy Spirit.

3.

O ALMIGHTY God, who art greatly to be feared in Thy holiness, we are ashamed of our manifold iniquities; we confess unto Thee our sin. We offend continually and grievously in deed, in word, and in thought. Our fathers have transgressed against Thee; and we, our children, and our brethren, do fill up the measure of their iniquity. We harden our hearts, and are impenitent; we are proud and rebellious; we are high-minded, and refuse to be humbled; we have lived in strife and confusion, and have not desired peace; we have loved lies and vanity, hypocrisy and deceit; we covet and lust after the things which perish, and seek not Thy heavenly kingdom.

4.

ALMIGHTY God, the Father of our Lord Jesus Christ, who hast given us grace at this time to confess our sins unto Thee, for the sake of Jesus Christ have mercy upon us; grant unto us full remission and forgiveness, and absolve us from all our sins, iniquities, and transgressions; grant unto us peace through Thy Word of pardon proclaimed unto us in His name; and vouchsafe unto us the inspiration of Thy Holy Spirit, that at this time present we may offer unto Thee true and acceptable worship; that for the time to come we may serve and please Thee, in newness of life, in righteousness and true holiness; and that at the coming of our Lord Jesus Christ we may be found of Him in peace unto salvation.

Visit and cleanse our consciences, we beseech Thee, O Lord, that when Thy Son our Lord Jesus Christ shall come He may find us fit and ready for His appearing.

Hasten, O God, the time when Thou shalt send from Thy right hand Him whom Thou wilt send; at whose glorious appearing Thy saints departed shall be raised, and we which are alive shall be caught up to meet Him, and so shall ever be with Him. Under the veil of earthly things we have now communion with Him; but with unveiled faces we shall then behold Him, rejoicing in His presence, made like unto Him in His glory; and by Him, with all Thy Church holy and unspotted, shall be presented before the presence of Thy glory with exceeding joy. Hear us, O heavenly Father, for His sake; to whom, with Thee and the Holy Ghost, one living and true God, be glory for ever and ever.

5.

OUR Father which art in heaven, &c.
Amen.

PRAYER AFTER LESSONS.

1.

WE give thanks unto Thee, O God of our salvation, that Thou hast crowned our lives with mercies; we look unto Thee as the Saviour and benefactor of our souls. Thou hast given us rest during the past night, and hast raised us from our beds in strength, and brought us to the worship of Thine adorable name: wherefore we worship Thee, O God. Bless us, and enable us to sing to Thee as we ought with the understanding, and without ceasing to pray to Thee, working out, with the help of Thy

Christ, our salvation with fear and trembling. For Thou art the Prince of peace, and Saviour of our souls, and to Thee we ascribe all glory.

Thou didst create heaven and earth, and all things that are therein. Thou gavest unto us life and being. By Thy providence are the fruits of the earth preserved to us; and by Thy blessing we, and all things living, are nourished and sustained. Thou openest Thine hand and fillest us with plenty. Thou hast preserved us all our days, and now again Thou bringest us into Thy presence, satisfied with Thy mercies, and replenished with Thy goodness.

Blessed be the Lord, who daily loadest us with benefits, even the God of our salvation. He that is our God is the God of salvation; and unto God the Lord belong the issues from death.

Glory be to God on high, and in earth peace, goodwill towards men. We praise Thee, we bless Thee, we worship Thee, we glorify Thee, we give thanks to Thee for Thy great glory, O Lord God, heavenly King, God the Father Almighty.

O Lord, the only-begotten Son, Jesus Christ; O Lamb of God, that takest away the sins of the world, have mercy upon us. Thou that takest away the sins of the world, have mercy upon us: Thou that takest away the sins of the world, receive our prayer: Thou that sittest at the right hand of God the Father, have mercy upon us.

For Thou only art holy; Thou only art the Lord; Thou only, O Christ, with the Holy Ghost, art most high in the glory of God the Father.

2.

O LORD our God, who hast shown great mercy to us, Thy sinful and unworthy servants, upon whom Thy holy name is called, put us not to shame for our hope in Thy mercy; but grant us, Lord, all these our petitions for salvation, and count us worthy to love and fear Thee with all our hearts, and to do in all things Thy most holy will. For Thou, O God, art good, and lovest all mankind. And to Thee we ascribe all glory, to the Father, and to the Son, and to the Holy Ghost, now and for evermore.

Amen.

THIRD PRAYER AFTER SERMON.

1.

ALMIGHTY and ever-living God, we draw near in the name of Thy Son Jesus Christ, our High Priest and Mediator, who hath passed into the heavens, where He abideth at Thy right hand, and ever liveth to make intercession for us. We bring unto Thee the supplications of Thy people, and the prayers of Thy Church : and we beseech Thee that they may come up with acceptance as incense upon Thine altar, and that Thou wilt be favourable unto us, and answer us in peace.

2.

REMEMBER, O Lord, according to the greatness of Thy mercies, all Thy people ; all now with us worshipping before Thee ; all who are now in need of Thy help by land, by sea, and in all places of Thy dominion, and show unto them all Thy mercy; and grant that, being preserved in soul and body, we may glorify with all boldness Thy wonderful and blessed name of Father, Son, and Holy Ghost, now and for evermore.

Regard with Thy compassion those who are in bitterness because of their transgressions ; give unto them true contrition of heart ; restore unto them the joy of Thy salvation, and uphold them with Thy free Spirit.

Have mercy upon all who are oppressed of the devil. Disappoint, we beseech Thee, the cruel malice of the enemy, and deliver Thy redeemed from his power.

We pray Thee for all kings, princes, and governors, and for all the people; especially for Thy servant Queen VICTORIA, for her family and council, and for all the people of her realm.

Bless the arms of Christian nations, and do Thou favour the righteous cause; give unto them peace one with another; take away all ambition and wicked lusts, and all that should endanger or destroy godly concord; save us from bloodshed and confusion, and vouchsafe unto all Christian men to dwell together as brethren in unity and peace.

Stir up the hearts of Christian parents to bring up their children in the nurture and admonition of the Lord. May the young be in such wise prepared to fulfil their calling in this life, that they may not fail to adorn the doctrine of their God and Saviour in all things.

Send forth the news of Thy salvation unto the ends of the earth; and turn the hearts of all men, and fetch all Thine erring children home unto Thy fold.

We pray Thee for favourable weather, and that Thou wilt give us the fruits of the earth in due season. We beseech Thee for all who are in trouble, sorrow, need, sickness, or any other adversity.

We commend unto Thee all departing this life, and we beseech Thee to receive them to Thy rest.

Glory be unto the Father, and to the Son, and to the Holy Ghost.

As it was in the beginning, is now, and ever shall be, world without end.

Amen.

The Benediction.

THE grace of our Lord Jesus Christ, &c.

Amen.

SECOND EVENING SERVICE.

Opening Prayer.

I.

LORD, I have loved the habitation of Thy house, and the place where Thine honour dwelleth.

Wherefore we, receiving a kingdom which cannot be moved, let us have grace, whereby we may serve God acceptably with reverence and godly fear; for our God is a consuming fire.

2.

ALMIGHTY and ever-living God, who hast given unto Thy Son Jesus Christ power over all flesh, that He should give eternal life to as many as Thou hast given Him; and hast raised Him to Thy right hand, to be High Priest over the house of God, and the Angel and Mediator of the new covenant, ever present with Thy people; in His name we come before Thy holy altar, and make supplication unto Thee.

Hear, O most holy Lord God, the intercessions and prayers of Thy people which have been made to Thee this day in Thy holy Church. Let our prayer be set forth before Thee as incense, and the lifting up of our hands as the evening sacrifice.

3.

ALMIGHTY and most merciful Father, we acknowledge and bewail our manifold sins and wickedness which we from time to time, and especially in the course of the past day, most grievously have committed, by thought, word, and deed, against Thy divine majesty, provoking most justly Thy wrath and indignation against us. We have broken the vows made unto Thee in our baptism, wherein we were made members of the body of Thy Son, and partakers of Thy Holy Spirit; we have separated ourselves from one another, disregarding the unity of Thy holy Church; we have not held fast the hope of the coming and kingdom of our Lord, and we have not purified ourselves as He is pure; we have not worthily praised Thee for Thy goodness, nor rendered unto Thee the glory due unto Thy holy name.

4.

WE do earnestly repent, and are heartily sorry for, these our misdoings. Have mercy upon us, have mercy upon us, most merciful Father; for Thy Son our Lord Jesus Christ's sake, forgive us all that is past, and especially the sins of this day; and grant that we may ever hereafter serve and please Thee in newness of life, to the honour and glory of Thy name.

Almighty God, our most merciful Father, who despisest not the sighing of the contrite heart, nor the desire of such as be sorrowful; who hast given Thine only-begotten Son to die for our sins, and for His sake takest not vengeance on them, but hast respect unto the blood of the Lamb which taketh away the sin of the world; pardon and forgive our innumerable offences committed against Thy divine majesty, and blot out as a thick cloud the transgressions of Thy Church, and remember no more her sins.

O Almighty God, who by Thy holy Apostles hast called upon us to present our bodies unto Thee a living sacrifice, holy and acceptable, which is our reasonable service; we come unto Thee in the name of Jesus Christ, and we devote and dedicate ourselves wholly to Thy service, henceforth to live only to Thy glory. Thou art our God, and we will praise Thee; Thou art our God, we will exalt Thee; we give thanks unto Thee, O Lord, for Thou art good, and Thy mercy endureth for ever.

O Almighty God, grant that those necessary works wherein we are engaged, whether in the affairs of Thy Church or of this world, may not avail to hinder us; but that, at the appearing and advent of Thy Son, we may hasten with joy to meet Him, who liveth and reigneth with Thee and the Holy Ghost, ever one God, world without end.

5.

OUR Father which art in heaven, &c.
Amen.

Third Prayer after Lessons.

O THOU whom cherubim and seraphim continually do praise, the heavens and all the powers therein; open Thou our mouths, that we may show forth Thy praise, and declare the greatness of Thy holy name. Grant unto us to have our portion with them who fear Thee in truth, and who obey Thy commandments; for to Thee is due all glory, honour, worship, Father, Son, and Holy Ghost, throughout all ages.

O God Most High, who alone art exalted, having immortality, and dwelling in the light which no man can approach unto; Thou hast made all things by Thy wisdom, separating between the light and the darkness, setting the sun to rule the day, and the moon to rule the night. Thou hast given us grace to come before Thee at this time, to offer unto Thee our evening song of adoration and praise; grant unto us peace for the present evening and coming night; clothe us with the armour of light; and being enlightened by Thy law, give us with joy to persevere in glorifying Thy goodness, offering prayers and supplications to Thy compassion for our fellow-sinners, and for all Thy people : which do Thou grant, according to Thy goodwill towards men.

We remember in Thy presence all for whom

we should beseech Thee, that they may receive the dew of Thy blessing, and the outpouring of Thy Holy Spirit. Revive us, O God; revive Thy Church, we pray Thee; have mercy upon all Thy creatures of mankind; gather all who shall be saved into Thy fold; bring in the fulness of the Gentiles; accomplish the number of Thine elect; and unite and carry onward to perfection all Thy saints. Grant unto Thy servants who shall depart in the faith, rest, and joy, and peace, in the hope of a blessed resurrection; and hasten the appearing and kingdom of our Lord and Saviour Jesus Christ.

These things we ask, O heavenly Father, in patient confidence and joyful hope, being assured that we ask them according to Thy will; that the voice of Thy Church is heard by Thee, that the intercessions of the Holy Ghost are known unto Thee, and that the mediation of Thy well-beloved Son, our Lord and Saviour, doth prevail with Thee.

Wherefore we glorify Thy name, we fall down before Thy throne, we worship and adore Thy glorious majesty; evermore praising Thee, and saying, Salvation be unto our God which sitteth upon the Throne, and unto the Lamb for ever. Blessing, and glory, and wisdom, and thanksgiving, and honour, and power, and might, be unto our God for ever and ever.

Amen.

Prayer after Sermon.

1.

O ALMIGHTY and most merciful Father, who hast loved Thine elect with an everlasting love, and purchased them unto Thyself with the blood of Thy dear Son; favourably regard, we beseech Thee, Thy flock and congregation, and confirm them evermore with all spiritual gifts. And grant that the whole company of the faithful may abide steadfast in the faith, abounding in hope, of one heart and of one mind, and filled with joy and with the Holy Ghost.

2.

HOLY Father, keep through Thine own name those whom Thou hast chosen in Christ Jesus; preserve them from the evil that is in the world; sanctify them through Thy truth; let Thy love be manifested in them; fill them with Thy Holy Spirit, that they may be one in Thee, O Father, and in Jesus Christ Thy Son; perfect them in the hope of His coming; give unto them a full entrance into His eternal kingdom, and make them partakers of His glory.

O Lord, be Thou exalted among all nations.

Let all kings fall down before Thee, let all nations serve Thee. In every place let incense and a pure offering be offered unto Thy name, and let the whole earth be filled with Thy glory.

Almighty and everlasting God, we are taught by Thy holy Word that the hearts of kings are in Thy rule and governance, and that Thou dost dispose and turn them as it seemeth best to Thy godly wisdom; we humbly beseech Thee so to dispose and govern the hearts of all Thy servants (and especially of Thy servant VICTORIA, our Queen and Governor), that in all their thoughts, words, and works, they may ever seek Thy honour and glory, and study to preserve Thy people committed to their charge, in wealth, peace, and godliness. Grant this, O merciful Father, for Thy dear Son's sake.

O Lord, govern us, we beseech Thee, by Thine own almighty power in all things; be Thou long-suffering with all of us, and turn unto us according to our supplications; remember Thy tenderness and Thy mercy; visit us in Thy goodness; and grant us by Thy blessing to escape through the remainder of this day the manifold wiles of the wicked one, and preserve our life from all snares by the grace of Thy most Holy Spirit.

Remember all who call to Thee in the night season; hear them, and have mercy upon them.

and cast their invisible and cruel enemy down under their feet.

Grant unto us to see the morning and the day in joy, that we may direct our morning prayers unto Thee, through Jesus Christ our Lord; for Thine is the dominion, the power, and the glory, world without end.
Amen.

The Benediction.

THE grace of our Lord Jesus Christ, and the love of God, and the communion of the Holy Ghost, be with you all.
Amen.

Sacrament of Baptism.

THE idea in the construction of the following Service has been to exhibit, first of all, the Scriptural warrant for the reception of children, in the words of Christ, which, accordingly, are read as the preface to that which follows. Immediately thereafter come, as is enjoined in the Westminster Directory, "some words of instruction touching the institution, nature, use, and ends of this sacrament." In these, while on the one hand the doctrine of Baptismal Regeneration is disclaimed, so on the other is distinctly set forth the doctrine of the Scottish, as of the whole Reformed, Church—that Baptism is not a mere sign, but (in the words of the Directory), "a seal of the covenant of grace, of our ingrafting into Christ, and of our union with Him; of remission of sins, regeneration, adoption, and life eternal." The same truth is recognised in the prayers that follow—it being the plain doctrine both of the Westminster Confession and of the Scottish Confession of 1560, which latter emphatically states: "we utterly condemn the vanity of those that affirm sacraments to be nothing else but naked and bare signs;" and again, "whosoever slandereth us that we affirm and believe sacraments to be such, doth injury unto us, and speaketh against the manifest truth."

The vow or declaration demanded of the parent or sponsor is simply a profession of belief in the Apostles' Creed, this being the profession required by the Church after the Reformation, and earnestly contended for by the Scottish Commissioners in the Westminster Assembly; and he is likewise bound to undertake that the child shall, if spared, be duly instructed. This part of the Service is very much akin to that found in the Baptismal Service of the "Savoy Liturgy." The prayer which follows upon it is taken very closely from the suggestions of the Directory.

The prayer after the act of Baptism is in accordance with the same authority, but it includes two topics not referred to therein—viz., the mother of the child, and both the parents and their family collectively; the paragraphs relative to which can be omitted when not appropriate. The Service concludes with the Lord's Prayer and the Apostolic Benediction.

This Baptismal Service, it will thus be seen, is compiled on the principle of carrying out, as closely as is consistent with the proper liberty left to the Minister by the Directory, the suggestions of that authority. If, on the one hand, a service drawn up on this principle lacks some of the tone and substance of the older and catholic formulas, it possesses, on the other hand, a simplicity and coherence, and a doctrinal distinctness, which are occasionally awanting in the baptismal services of those who do not even avail themselves of those directions which they yet profess to regard as their rule and standard.*

* It is assumed that the father appears as sponsor for the child (but the Directory provides for the necessary absence of that parent by admitting a "Christian friend" as sponsor), and that the baptism takes place in the church, as the Directory requires.

Administration of Baptism to Infants.

When the Father, or other Sponsor, with the Mother, if she be present, has stood up in the place appointed, presenting the child, the Minister shall say:

Do you present this child to God in the holy sacrament of Baptism?
Ans.—We do.

Then the Minister shall say:

It is written in the 10th chapter of the Gospel according to S. Mark, at the 13th verse: "They brought young children to Him, that He should touch them: and His disciples rebuked those that brought them. But when Jesus saw it, He was much displeased, and said unto them, Suffer the little children to come unto me, and forbid them not: for of such is the kingdom of God. Verily I say unto you, Whosoever shall not receive the kingdom of God as a little child, he shall not enter therein. And He took them up in His arms, put His hands upon them, and blessed them."

Let us not doubt, dearly beloved, but firmly believe that the same loving Saviour who is ever present in His Church will now receive and bless this little one whom you now dedicate to Him, and will show His abundant mercy unto us and to our children.

The Minister shall then instruct the Sponsor thus:

To present their children unto God in Baptism is the bounden duty and the high privilege of Christians, who, themselves members of the body of Christ, believe their children to be the heritage of the Lord, and recognise it to be their part to train them up as members of the great family in earth and heaven which has been redeemed by the precious blood of Christ: for in this holy sacrament we are taught that we are not our own, but are bought with a price, and must therefore be devoted in soul and body to the Lord; and also, that being in ourselves unclean, we must be sprinkled with the Saviour's blood ere we can be an acceptable people in God's sight. And although the water of Baptism cannot in itself avail to the washing away of sin or the regeneration of the soul, yet therein are signified and sealed unto us our ingrafting into the body of Christ, and the promise of His Spirit, who only can cleanse and sanctify the spirit that is in man.

You have heard how the blessed Lord said in the days of His flesh, " Suffer the little children to come unto me, and forbid them not, for of such is the kingdom of God ;" and therefore, although children be unable to take upon themselves the vows of the Lord, it is our duty to present them unto God in Baptism—even as under the Law of Moses our Lord himself was presented for circumcision—in order that they may receive the seal of the covenant, and be admitted in Christ's name into the fold of His Church, to be trained for His heavenly kingdom.

Or thus:

The holy ordinance of Baptism was instituted by the Lord Jesus Christ, who, before He left this world, spake unto His disciples, saying: "All power is given unto me in heaven and in earth. Go ye therefore and teach all nations, baptizing them in the name of the Father, and of the Son, and of the Holy Ghost; teaching them to observe all things whatsoever I have commanded you; and, lo, I am with you alway, even unto the end of the world."

The sacrament thus instituted is a holy sign and seal of the covenant of grace, of our ingrafting into Christ and union with Him, of remission of sins, regeneration, adoption, and life eternal. This element of water representeth both the blood of Christ, which taketh away all the guilt of sin, and the power of the Holy Ghost in regenerating and sanctifying our corrupt nature. And as by Baptism we are solemnly received into the Church, we are taught, and acknowledge thereby, that all men are born in sin, and must be cleansed by Christ's blood and Spirit, if they would be accepted of God and admitted to His heavenly kingdom. The baptism of water cannot of itself effect that which it signifies; but as it is a sign appointed by divine wisdom to show us our need of heavenly cleansing, so is it also a seal whereby God confirms to all who are baptized His promise to bestow it; assuring them thereby of His goodwill and love, ingrafting them into the body of Christ, receiving them into His household, and giving them a covenant right to look to Him as their Father, and to expect through faith all the blessings of salvation.

On the other part, all who by Baptism are admitted to these inestimable privileges, do thereby renounce the devil, the world, and the flesh, the enemies of God and of their souls, and come under a covenant obligation to place all their hope of salvation in Christ alone; they become bound to believe God's Word, to obey His commandments, and to live as heirs of His heavenly kingdom, to the glory of His holy name.

Then he shall add:

As you desire this child to be received into the fellowship of the faith, it is necessary that you profess that faith into which *he* is to be baptized, and promise that *he* shall be trained in the knowledge and obedience of the truth. I therefore ask you before God and these witnesses—Do you believe in God the Father Almighty, maker of heaven and earth; and in Jesus Christ, His only Son, our Lord; who was conceived by the Holy Ghost; born of the Virgin Mary; suffered under Pontius Pilate; was crucified, dead, and buried: that He descended into hell; that the third day He rose again from the dead; that He ascended into heaven; and sitteth on the right hand of God the Father Almighty; that from thence He shall come to judge the quick and the dead? Do you believe in the Holy Ghost; the holy catholic Church; the communion of saints; the forgiveness of sins; the resurrection of the body; and the life everlasting?

Ans.—We do.

Minister.—Do you promise that if it shall please God to spare this child, you shall, as soon as *he* is able to understand them, instruct *him* [or cause *him* to be instructed] in these truths, and in the meaning of the baptismal covenant; and according to your best ability, by good example, and with prayer to God on *his* behalf, train *him* up in the nurture and admonition of the Lord?

Ans.—We do.

Minister.—The Lord preserve you and this child and give you grace to fulfil your vow.

SACRAMENT OF BAPTISM.

Let us pray.

ALMIGHTY God, our heavenly Father, who hast made Thy Son Jesus Christ to be Head over all things to the Church, which is His body, and who, through Him, didst deliver this command to the first ministers and stewards of Thy word and sacraments, " Go ye and teach all nations, baptizing them in the name of the Father, and of the Son, and of the Holy Ghost ;" giving unto them also through the same Jesus Christ our Lord this promise, " Lo, I am with you alway, even unto the end of the world ;" we beseech Thee to fulfil this Thy promise unto us, as we now obey this Thy command, and graciously to be with us as we receive this little child into the fold of the holy catholic Church. May it please Thee to sanctify this element of water to this spiritual use ; and to join the inward baptism of Thy Spirit to the outward baptism of water, making it to this child the seal of remission of sins, of adoption, regeneration, and eternal life; so that the body of sin and death being destroyed in *him*, *he* may walk henceforth in newness of life, through Jesus Christ *his* Lord.

Amen.

Or as follows:

ALMIGHTY and everlasting God, who of Thine infinite mercy and goodness hast promised unto us that Thou wilt be not only our God, but also the God and Father of our children, We pray Thee, that as thou hast vouchsafed to call us to be partakers of this Thy great mercy in the fellowship of faith, so it may please Thee to sanctify with Thy Spirit, and to receive into the number of Thy children, this infant whom we—beseeching Thee to sanctify this water which we use in obedience to our Lord's appointment—are about to baptize according to Thy word; to the end that *he*, coming to mature age, may confess Thee the only true God, and Jesus Christ whom thou hast sent; and may serve Thee, and be profitable unto Thy Church, all the days of *his* life; so that, after this life is ended, *he* may be brought, as a living member of Thy Son's body, unto the full fruition of Thy joys in heaven, where our Saviour Christ reigneth with Thee the Father, in the unity of the Spirit, world without end.

Amen.

Then the Father or Sponsor, presenting the child at the font or laver (the Congregation standing), the Minister shall say:

Name this child.
Ans.—*M.* [or *N.*]

SACRAMENT OF BAPTISM. 195

Then the Minister, naming the child by name, shall pour or sprinkle water upon the child's face, saying:

M. [or *N.*] I baptize thee in the name of the Father, and of the Son, and of the Holy Ghost.

𝔄men.

Then the Minister may add:

The Lord bless thee and keep thee. The Lord make His face to shine upon thee, and be gracious unto thee. The Lord lift up His countenance upon thee, and give thee peace.

𝔄men.

𝔏et us pray.

ALMIGHTY God, merciful Father, we beseech Thee to seal with Thy blessing that which has now been done in Thy name, and by Thine authority. May it please Thee to give unto This child a new name written in the Lamb's book of life, and a place in Thy heavenly temple, whence *he* shall go no more out. Do Thou take *him* into Thy fatherly care and keeping, and regard *him* with the favour which Thou bearest unto Thine own children. Grant to *him*, if it be Thy loving will, health of body and soundness of mind ; save *him* from all evil and mischief in soul and body ; may *he*, like Thy holy child Jesus, grow in wisdom as *he* grows in stature, and in favour with God and man; may *he* be kept by Thy mighty power—who willest not that one of those little ones should perish—through faith unto salvation; and after the trials and changes, the joys and sorrows, of this transitory life are over, may *he* inherit Thy promises, and enter into Thy blessed rest, through Jesus Christ *his* Lord.

[O Lord, who redeemest our life from destruction, and crownest us with loving-kindness and tender mercy, we offer unto Thee our thanksgivings on behalf of the mother of this child: in that Thou hast been pleased to spare her to rejoice over her little one. Be Thou at all times her refuge and her strength, and finally may she inherit Thine eternal kingdom, through Jesus Christ her Lord.]

[Hear our prayers, we beseech Thee, O God, on behalf of the parents of this child: that Thou wouldst graciously spare *them* to rule *their family* in Thy fear and love. Bless *them* in all *their* worldly concerns: grant unto *them* all spiritual blessings in heavenly places in Christ Jesus. Enlighten *them* in the knowledge of Thy will, that *they* may be enabled to bring up this child [and all the children that Thou givest *them*] in the fear of the Lord, which is the beginning of wisdom. And do Thou so guide and govern *them* by Thy good Spirit, that in this world *they* may together glorify Thy name by a devout walk and conversation ; and in the world to come may be numbered with Thy saints in the glory everlasting, having finally been presented faultless before the presence of Thy glory with exceeding joy, through Jesus Christ our Lord.]

OUR Father which art in heaven, Hallowed be thy name. Thy kingdom come. Thy will be done in earth, as it is in heaven. Give us this day our daily bread. And forgive us our debts, as we forgive our debtors. And lead us not into temptation, but deliver us from evil : For Thine is the kingdom, and the power, and the glory, for ever.
Amen.

THE grace of the Lord Jesus Christ, and the love of God, and the communion of the Holy Ghost, be with you all.
Amen.

Admission of Young Persons to the Lord's Supper.

In all Protestant Churches infant communion was discontinued, chrism was swept away, and there was substituted for it the confirmation of the baptismal vow by the baptized on coming to years of discretion, and before admission to the Lord's Supper.

We shall give some specimens of the way in which this service is conducted in Protestant Churches.

The Church of England.

The Articles of this Church say of the ante-Reformation confirmation, that it had "grown of the corrupt following of the Apostles, and had no visible sign or ceremony ordained of God." A new service was accordingly introduced, which prescribes that none are to be confirmed till they come to years of discretion, have been instructed in the Creed and Catechism, and can answer for themselves. It contains also a distinct confirmation of the baptismal vow. It is not administered, however, except by prelates; and, instead of chrism, the supposed post-Apostolic practice of laying on of hands is followed. Bunsen says that Anglican confirmation is, "as to its essence and efficacy, an *opus operatum.*" Certainly there is something of the same double aspect about it which characterizes other parts of the liturgy; and some Anglican writers try to identify it with the anointing of infants, as practised for so many ages. But for this, the service would be simple and appropriate.

THE CHURCH OF GENÉVA.

In Geneva special religious instruction for the communion lasts for a year. It begins with girls at the age of fifteen, with young men at the age of sixteen, who meet with the pastor twice a-week. When prepared, their admission takes place as follows:—

After sermon on the day of preparation for the Communion,

I. The pastor gives a short address to the congregation and to the catechumens.

II. He then puts the following questions:—

(1.) Catechumens who present yourselves to

be admitted to the Lord's Supper, do you sincerely believe in the truths of the Gospel, and are you so firmly convinced of these truths that you are ready to suffer the loss of all things, rather than abandon your Christian profession?

(2.) Do you desire to respond to the love that God hath shown to you in Jesus Christ, by loving the Lord your God with all your heart, with all your soul, and with all your mind?

(3.) Are you desirous of loving your neighbour as yourselves, and of living with your brethren in peace, in charity, and in the communion of Jesus?

(4.) Are you resolved, in reliance upon the aid of the Holy Spirit, to fight against sin, and to regulate your lives by the commands of God?

(5.) For the strengthening of your faith and piety, do you promise to apply yourselves to prayer, to read with care the Word of God, and assiduously to frequent the holy assemblies?

(6.) Do you declare, in the sight of God, and in the presence of the Church, that you confirm the vow of your Baptism, and that you consecrate yourselves to God your Father, and to Jesus Christ your Saviour?

III. These questions having been answered, the pastor says:—"In consequence of these declarations and promises, I admit you, in the name of the Lord, to partake of the Holy Supper, and of all the privileges of the new covenant which God hath made with us through his Son." He then gives an address to them and to the congregation.

IV. Prayer of thanks and for grace, concluding, as at an ordinary service, with the Intercessory Prayer, Lord's Prayer, and Creed.

V. Praise.

VI. Benediction.

The French and Waldensian services for the reception of catechumens are substantially the same as the Genevan.

The Church of Neufchatel.

At Neufchatel the catechumens make the following promise in the face of the Church :—

"We ratify and confirm the vow of our Baptism. We renounce the devil and his works, the world and its pomp, the flesh and its lusts. We promise to live and to die in the Christian faith, and to keep the commandments of God all the time of our life."

This is followed by the formula of admission, the address, prayer, and benediction.

The Dutch Church.

In Holland catechumens are instructed for years in the Confession of Faith, Heidelberg Catechism, Bible history, and history of the Reformation; and, when about eighteen, are publicly received on one of the days of worship preparatory to the Lord's Supper. The ceremony is called confirmation. They are prayed for by the pastor, and are asked:—" Whether they confess and are satisfied with the fundamental truths of the Gospel, as set forth in the Catechisms of the Church? Whether they have experienced the power of the truth in their hearts, and are willing and desirous to be saved by Jesus Christ from their sins? and whether they propose, by the grace of God, to persevere in this doctrine, to forsake the world, and to lead a new Christian life? Lastly, Whether they will submit themselves to the Christian discipline? Which being done, they are to be exhorted to peace, love, and concord with all men, and to reconciliation, if there is any variance subsisting, between them and their neighbours."

AMERICAN GERMAN REFORMED CHURCH.

In the provisional liturgy of this Church, designed to supersede the old Church books as used by the Reformed in Germany, the confirmation service is as follows:—

At the time appointed the minister reads the names of the catechumens, who then come forward.

(1.) Benediction.

(2.) Address—setting forth that the service is a following of the example of the apostles; that by it baptized children are fully consecrated to the Christian priesthood; and that, while they ratify the promises of their Baptism, "the Church in God's stead imparts unto them in larger measure the Holy Ghost."

(3.) Questions:—(*a*) Do you now, in the presence of God and of this congregation, renew the solemn promise and vow made in your name at your Baptism? Do you ratify and confirm the same, and acknowledge yourself bound to believe and to do all those things which your parents then undertook for you? (*b*) Do you renounce the devil, with all his ways and works — the world, with its vain pomp and glory—and the flesh, with all its sinful desires? (*c*) Profess now your faith before God and this congregation. (The catechumens here repeat the Apostle's Creed.)

(4.) Prayer for the Holy Ghost and His manifold gifts.

The catechumens then kneel, and the pastor blesses each successively, with imposition of hands.

Prayer of thanks and for grace.

(5.) Address to the congregation, commending those who have been confirmed to their Christian sympathy and regard.

(6.) Benediction.

The Church of Scotland.

The First Book of Discipline says that "none are to be admitted to the mystery (the Lord's Supper) who cannot formally say the Lord's Prayer, the Articles of Belief, nor declare the sum of the law;" also that, "every year at the least, public examination be had by the ministers and elders of the knowledge of every person in the Kirk."

There was at this period no regulation as to the manner of admitting young people to the Communion. The idea seems to have prevailed that they should communicate very early. James Melville did so, he tells us, at the age of thirteen. The annual examination obviously took the place of the annual private confession before the Reformation.

In 1618 prelatical confirmation was enjoined by the Articles of Perth, but was seldom or never practised. In 1641 Henderson says, in his "Government and Order of the Church of Scotland," that "none are admitted to the Lord's Supper but such as, upon examination, are found to have a competent measure of knowledge in the grounds of the Christian religion, and the doctrine of the Sacraments, and are able, according to the Apostle's commandment, and profess themselves willing, to examine themselves, and to renew their covenant made with God in Baptism, promising to walk as beseemeth Christians, and to submit themselves to all the ordinances of Christ."

At Westminster the subject was passed over in very general terms, partly on account of the discord between the Independents and Presbyterians as to the qualifications for Church membership. This led to a defect which has been felt wherever the Westminster Standards have been received.

At the Restoration, a few years after the Assembly, the English Presbyterian divines, in their negotiations as to the Church, required "that none should be admitted to the . . . Lord's Supper, till they have . . . understood the meaning of their baptismal covenant; and with their own mouths, and their own consent, openly before the Church, ratified and confirmed, and also promised that, by the grace of God, they will evermore endeavour themselves faithfully to observe and keep such things as . . . they have assented to." . . . "Unless it be in case of some extraordinary natural imperfection and inability of utterance, let him (they say) at least openly recite the Creed, and profess his consent to the covenant with God the Father, Son, and Holy Ghost."

In the Form of Process, or Book of Discipline, which, after the Revolution, occupied the attention of several General Assemblies, and which was printed for transmission to Presbyteries in 1704, there is the following regulation :—" At the first admission of any to the Lord's Supper, ministers should put the persons to be admitted in mind of their parents' engagements for them in Baptism, and put them, explicitly and personally, to renew their baptismal covenant to be the Lord's, and to live unto Him, and serve Him, all the days of their lives." In 1706 the Assembly passed an Act to this effect.

The want of something more definite has, however, given rise to a great variety of practice, and the intention of the Church is not always carried out.

In the American Presbyterian Church an addition is made to the Directory, with the view of supplying the defect in the Westminster Standards; and in some of the colonial offshoots from Scottish Presbyterianism, questions are prescribed to be put, in the face of the congregation, to young people before admission to the Lord's Supper.

These specimens are sufficient to show what "confirmation" is in Protestant Churches, and what the principal ideas are that should enter into a form for the reception of catechumens.

"Confirmation," in the sense of one's confirming his baptismal vow, is the invariable complement of infant Baptism. The whole practical system of the Church is based on the baptismal covenant entered by the child and accepted by the young person.

Preparation for this service, and the occasion itself, should be made much of, as there is no other season so powerful for good among the young, when rightly utilised.

The reception of the catechumens should take place in the presence of the whole congregation. It is the owning of their Baptism, their great public profession of faith in the Saviour, their solemn admission to full membership in the Church; so that all reasons for public Baptism in the case of adults apply also to it.

They should be asked such questions as the following:—If they believe the articles of the Creed? if they own and confirm their Baptism? if they are resolved to renounce sin and keep God's commandments? if they will submit to the discipline of the Church, abide in its fellowship, and give for the extension of the Gospel as God may prosper them? These things are involved in Church membership; and if they were made more prominent, people would have a better idea than they have of their obligations as Christians.

These questions being answered, the pastor, on behalf of the Church, should solemnly admit them to full membership, counsel them, and in prayer thank God for having spared them to profess their faith in Christ, and ask His grace and the aids of His Spirit to strengthen them for the Christian warfare. They should also be solemnly blessed. Calvin said,—" The laying on of hands, which is done simply by way of benediction, I commend, and would like to see restored to its pure use in the present day." This is no doubt the proper gesture of blessing, when it is possible to use it. In other cases the lifting up and stretching forth of the hands should take its place.

We give the following as a specimen of such a service, compiled chiefly from the Reformed Liturgies:—

Admission of Catechumens.

On the day of preparation for the Lord's Supper, the Pastor, after the ordinary sermon and the constituting of the Session, shall say:

Dearly beloved,—We are now about to admit to full membership in the Church, and to the participation of the Lord's Supper, the catechumens who have been under special instruction in the truths of the Gospel, and who are ready to profess publicly the faith into which they were baptized.

The Minister shall then read their names, and they will come forward and stand in front of the pulpit.

Addressing the Catechumens, the Minister shall say:

Dearly beloved,—In the days of your infancy you were by Holy Baptism ingrafted into the Lord Jesus Christ, and engaged to be His. God, in His mercy, has spared you to years of responsibility; and you have now, of your own choice, come forward to own and accept, before God and His Church, the covenant then made on your behalf—to profess your faith in the Lord Jesus—to consecrate yourselves to Him, and thereby to release your sureties, and bind yourselves anew to His service.

This is one of the most solemn acts in the Christian's life. I charge you, therefore, to answer with all sincerity, and as in the presence of God, who sees your hearts, the questions which I have now to put to you.

1. Do you believe in God the Father Almighty, Maker of heaven and earth; and in Jesus Christ, His only Son, our Lord; who was conceived by the Holy Ghost; born of the Virgin Mary; suffered under Pontius Pilate; was crucified, dead, and buried: that He descended into hell; that the third day He rose again from the dead; that He ascended into heaven, and sitteth on the right hand of God the Father Almighty; that from thence He shall come to judge the quick and the dead? Do you believe in the Holy Ghost; the holy catholic Church; the communion of saints; the forgiveness of sins; the resurrection of the body; and the life everlasting? These articles of the Christian faith, and the whole doctrine of the Old and New Testaments, you profess to believe: do you not? *Ans.—* I do.

2. Relying upon the help of the Holy Spirit, do you promise to renounce sin, and to regulate your lives by the commandments of God? *Ans.—*I do.

3. Do you promise to use faithfully the means of grace, the Word, sacraments, and prayer; and to give for the relief of the poor, and the extension of the Church, as the Lord may prosper you? *Ans.—*I do.

4. Finally, do you sincerely confirm the vow of your Baptism, and consecrate yourselves to God as your Father, to Christ as your Saviour, and to the Holy Ghost as your Sanctifier? *Ans.*—I do.

In consequence of these declarations and promises, and being satisfied as to your Baptism, your Christian knowledge and life, I, on behalf of the Church, do, in the name of our Lord Jesus Christ, admit you to the participation of the Lord's Supper, and to all the privileges of the new covenant.

The very God of peace sanctify you wholly: And I pray God your whole spirit, and soul, and body, be preserved blameless unto the coming of our Lord Jesus Christ.

Let us Pray.

ALMIGHTY God, who hast formed a Church in the world, and hast promised to perpetuate and protect it to the end of time, we thank Thee for Thy great mercy to these Thy children, and to Thy Church, to which Thou hast given the joy of receiving them into full communion. We thank Thee that from infancy, by Holy Baptism, they have been incorporated into the kingdom of Christ. We thank Thee for their Christian education—for the exhortation of parents and teachers—and that Thou hast spared them, and given them power this day to own and accept for themselves the covenant of salvation made with them before in the sacrament of Baptism. Forgive, O Lord, all the sins which they, in the foolishness of youth, have committed against Thee; and graciously accept them now dedicating themselves to Thee their Lord and God. Send down upon them the Holy Spirit the Comforter, and daily increase in them the manifold gifts of Thy grace, the spirit of wisdom and understanding, the spirit of counsel and might, the spirit of knowledge and of the fear of the Lord. As they have vowed to be Thy servants, help them, Lord, to fulfil their vow, and to remain faithful to Thee. May they bring forth abundantly the fruits of the Spirit, so that Thy Church and people may be comforted and strengthened through them. Defend them from all heresy and schism, from apostasy and unbelief. When they approach Thy holy table, to partake of the most precious body and blood of Christ, may they receive a rich measure of Thy grace. And grant, O most merciful Father, that they may continue steadfast unto the end, and that their portion may be with Thy saints at the second and glorious appearing of our Lord and Saviour Jesus Christ.

  Amen.

EXHORTATION.

Dearly beloved,—Your eternal welfare depends upon the way in which you fulfil the engagements that you have now undertaken. I beseech you therefore to remember them throughout your whole life. Admitted to the privilege of full membership in the Christian Church, walk worthy of your vocation. Fulfil your part as good soldiers of Christ, and strengthen your brethren, in whose ranks you now take your place. Remember that you are the temples of the Holy Ghost, and the members of Christ, and that you are bound to glorify Him with your bodies and spirits which he hath redeemed. Flee youthful lusts: give yourselves to piety, temperance, charity, and all the Christian graces. Obey those who are over you in the Lord; shun heresy and schism; and labour for the peace and prosperity of the Church.

That you may be enabled to be faithful, seek always the help of God; wait upon all His ordinances; live by His Word; and join watchfulness to prayer.

Thus devoting yourselves to your God and Saviour from your early years, you will find His yoke to be easy, and His burden light. God on His part will bless you. He will give you His peace which passeth all understanding.

He will make all things work together for your good, and you will finally receive the crown of life.

BENEDICTION.

THE grace of our Lord Jesus Christ, and the love of God, and the communion of the Holy Ghost, be with you all.

Amen.

The Sacrament of the Lord's Supper.

MATERIAL FOR A SERVICE HAVING GENERAL SANCTION.

1. The Offertory. Originally offerings were made from which the elements were provided; and from the first, alms have been given by common Christian consent at the Communion.

2. Bringing forward the elements at the commencement of the service, when the alms are collected.

3. The Creed. Given in substance in the earliest forms, it became common after A.D. 500, and has since been retained either in the service proper, or preparatory.

4. Prayer of confession and for worthiness. This is universal either in the Communion Office proper, or in the preparatory service.

5. Eucharistic Prayer or Preface, with Salutation, Sursum Corda, and Seraphic Hymn. The use of this has been universal from the beginning, except in some of the Reformed Services, and even in them the Sursum Corda occurs in the address.

6. Words of Institution, and Invocation of the Spirit. The latter is not given distinctly in the Roman Office, nor in the Anglican, nor in some of the Foreign Reformed; but it was universal of old, was considered essential, and is prescribed in our Directory.

7. Intercession for the Church Militant, and thanksgiving for the righteous departed,—the communion of saints being a prominent thought connected with the Lord's Supper. The intercession either forms part of the Communion Services, or of the prayers after sermon preparatory to the Communion.

8. The Lord's Prayer. Anciently this was said at the end of the prayers before the Communion, and the use of it in this way was probably apostolic.

9. Prayer, &c., and Sancta Sanctis.

10. Singing of psalms at intervals during the Communion, if there be more than one "Table."

11. Prayer of thanksgiving for the Sacrament, and of self-dedication.

12. Praise.

13. Benediction.

The Decalogue forms no part of any Communion Service except the Anglican. In the Reformed Liturgies, it is given in the early part of the ordinary church service in accordance with the words, "The law is our schoolmaster to bring us unto Christ;" and on days of Communion, if not on every Lord's Day, it should no doubt form part of the Scripture read. The use of it in the Anglican Communion Office was borrowed from the Continental reformers, but the responses are insular.

There are no exhortations in ancient forms, beyond a few words for the dismissal of catechumens; but in all the Reformed Services there is at least one exhortation of some length.

"Table Addresses" are alike unknown to the old forms and to the Reformed Services, beyond the optional use of a few words. In the Reformed Churches (both in those where sitting and in those where standing was adopted) it was designed that the people should come forward in companies, receive, and make room for others, singing going on in the interval, and no more time being occupied where sitting was the posture than where standing was adopted.

Omitting everything objectionable, the following material may be considered as common to all Christendom, and should have a place in every Communion Service : — The Offertory ; Bringing in of the Elements; Salutation; Creed; Confession and Prayer of Approach; Eucharistic Prayer, with Versicles and Seraphic Hymn ; Words of Institution ; Invocation and Lord's Prayer; Intercession for the Church Militant, and Thanksgiving for the Righteous Departed ; Communion; Prayer of Thanks for the Sacrament, and of Self-Dedication; Praise and Benediction.

To this it may be necessary to add an exhortation, or exhortations. The ancient Service was, however, purely devotional. Material for the exhortations is to be found in the Reformed Liturgies.

THE ORDER OF THE COMMUNION SERVICE.

The ancient Order, as given in the first definite account, that of the Apostolic Constitutions, still commends itself to most. According to it, the Eucharistic Prayer is followed by the Words of Institution and Invocation, and these (before Communion) by the Great Intercession. We follow, however, substantially the order of the Directory, wishing to adhere to the common usage. The outline of the Directory is better than that of most Post-Reformation Services, and in many respects resembles the unartificial forms of the primitive Church. The Intercession is placed in the Post-Communion Service, where it is unconnected with any suggestions of an Oblation, and where it may even be said to occur naturally, when we have partaken of "that bread" which unites us as members of the one body. The order adopted is as follows:—

After an exhortation before Communion,

Introductory
{ Offertory.
Elements brought forward.
Places taken,
35th Paraphrase being sung meanwhile. }

Institution
{ Minister's Salutation.
Words of Institution.
Address. }

FORMS OF WORSHIP.

Eucharistic Invocation, &c.
{ Profession of Faith.
Prayer of Access.
Eucharistic Prayer, with Seraphic Hymn.
Invocation of the Holy Spirit.
Lord's Prayer. }

COMMUNION.

Post-Communion
{ Exhortation to Thankfulness.
Prayer of Thanks, and Self-Dedication.
Great Intercession for the Living, and thanks for the Righteous Departed.
Praise—Song of Simeon.
Benediction. }

EXHORTATION BEFORE THE COMMUNION.

The Prayer after Sermon being ended, the Minister may give this Exhortation: *

Dearly beloved,—As we are now about to celebrate the Holy Communion of the body and blood of Christ, let us consider how S. Paul exhorteth all persons to examine themselves before

---

* This Exhortation is in accordance with the Directory, and being for the whole congregation, should be given from the pulpit. It answers to the Dismissal of the Catechumens in the Ancient Church. The first paragraph is from the Book of Common Order, and the English Prayer-Book, which here have the

they eat of that bread, and drink of that cup. For, as the benefit is great, if with a truly penitent heart, and lively faith, we receive that holy sacrament (for then we spiritually eat the flesh of Christ, and drink His blood; then we dwell in Christ and Christ in us, we are one with Christ and Christ with us), so is the danger great if we receive the same unworthily. For then we are guilty of the body and blood of Christ our Saviour; we eat and drink our own condemnation, not discerning the Lord's body.

Therefore, in the name of the eternal God, and of His Son Jesus Christ, I warn all who are not of the number of the faithful, all who live in any sin against their knowledge or their conscience, charging them that they profane not this holy table.

And yet this I pronounce, not to exclude any penitent person, how grievous soever his sins have been, but only such as continue in sin without repentance.

Examine your own consciences, therefore, to know whether you truly repent of your sins, and whether, trusting in God's mercy, and seeking your whole salvation in Jesus Christ, you are

same words. The rest, slightly shortened, and modernised, is from the Book of Common Order, and the other Reformed Services. The usual Reformed Exhortation has a second part, but the topics in it are more appropriate to the Communion Service proper. We have added the Sancta Sanctis of the Primitive Church, as suitable in this place.

resolved to follow holiness, and to live in peace and charity with all men.

If you have this testimony in your hearts before God, I bid you, in the name of our Lord Jesus Christ, to His holy table.

And although you feel that you have not perfect faith, and do not serve God with such zeal as you ought, but have daily to fight against the lusts of your flesh; yet if, by God's grace, you are heartily sorry for these weaknesses, and earnestly desire to withstand all unbelief, and to keep all His commandments, be assured that your remaining sins and infirmities do not prevent you from being received of God in mercy, and so made worthy partakers of this heavenly food.

For we come not to this Supper as righteous in ourselves, but we come to seek our life in Christ, acknowledging that we lie in the midst of death. Let us, then, look upon this sacrament as a remedy for those who are sick, and consider that the worthiness our Lord requireth of us is, that we be truly sorry for our sins, and find our joy and salvation in Him. United with Him who is holy, even our Lord Jesus Christ, we are accepted of the Father, and invited to partake of these HOLY THINGS WHICH ARE FOR HOLY PERSONS.

Or,

AS we are now about to celebrate the Holy Communion of the body and blood of Christ, let us consider how S. Paul exhorteth all persons to examine themselves before they eat of that bread and drink of that cup. For as the benefit is great, if with a truly penitent heart, and lively faith, we receive that holy sacrament (for then we spiritually eat the flesh of Christ and drink His blood; then we dwell in Christ and Christ in us, we are one with Christ and Christ with us), so is the danger great if we receive the same unworthily, for then are we guilty of the body and blood of the Lord.

Let us then examine ourselves as to our faith in the doctrines of the Gospel, set forth in the Apostle's Creed, as follows :—

I believe in God the Father Almighty, Maker of heaven and earth; and in Jesus Christ, His only Son, our Lord; who was conceived by the Holy Ghost; born of the Virgin Mary; suffered under Pontius Pilate; was crucified, dead, and buried. He descended into hell; the third day he rose again from the dead; he ascended into heaven, and sitteth on the right hand of God the Father Almighty; from thence he shall come to judge the quick and the dead. I believe in the Holy Ghost; the holy catholic Church; the communion of saints; the forgiveness of sins;

the resurrection of the body; and the life everlasting.

𝔄men.

But as "faith without works is dead, being alone," let us further examine ourselves whether we truly bear the Christian character, and are living the Christian life.

The Christian character is described by our Lord himself in the 5th chapter of S. Matthew, at the 3d verse, where we read:—

Blessed are the poor in spirit: for theirs is the kingdom of heaven.

Blessed are they that mourn: for they shall be comforted.

Blessed are the meek: for they shall inherit the earth.

Blessed are they which do hunger and thirst after righteousness: for they shall be filled.

Blessed are the merciful: for they shall obtain mercy.

Blessed are the poor in heart: for they shall see God.

Blessed are the peacemakers: for they shall be called the children of God.

Blessed are they which are persecuted for righteousness' sake: for theirs is the kingdom of heaven.

And the Christian life is set forth by S. Paul in his Epistle to the Galatians, in the 5th chapter, and at the 22d verse:—

But the fruit of the Spirit is love, joy, peace, longsuffering, gentleness, goodness, faith,

Meekness, temperance: against such there is no law.
And they that are Christ's have crucified the flesh with the affections and lusts.

Yet as we must all confess with sorrow that we have not lived thus, let us chiefly now remember the loving-kindness of the Saviour to all such as truly and heartily repented—how he turned not any away from him; how he blessed the woman which was a sinner, and gave to the penitent thief on the cross the assurance of Paradise.

Let us hear also what comfortable words our Saviour thus saith unto all that truly turn to Him :—

Come unto me, all ye that labour and are heavy laden, and I will give you rest.
Take my yoke upon you, and learn of me; for I am meek and lowly in heart: and ye shall find rest unto your souls.
For my yoke is easy, and my burden is light.

And—

All that the Father giveth me shall come to me; and him that cometh to me, I will in no wise cast out.

Hear also what S. Paul saith in his first Epistle to Timothy (1 Tim. i. 1 5) :—

This is a faithful saying, and worthy of all acceptation, that Christ Jesus came into the world to save sinners; of whom I am chief.

P

Hear also what S. John saith (1 John ii. 1) :—

If any man sin, we have an advocate with the Father, Jesus Christ the righteous :

And he is the propitiation for our sins ; and not for ours only, but also for the sins of the whole world.

Ye that do truly and earnestly repent you of your sins, and are in love and charity with your neighbours, and purpose to lead a new life, following the commandments of God, and walking from henceforth in His holy ways, draw near with faith and take this holy sacrament to your comfort, considering that the worthiness which the Lord requireth of us is, that we be truly sorry for our sins, and find our joy and salvation in Him. United to Him who is holy, even our Lord Jesus Christ, we are accepted of the Father, and invited to partake of those HOLY THINGS THAT ARE FOR HOLY PERSONS.

Then the Minister gives out a hymn (35th Paraphrase).

The Holy Communion.

While the hymn is being sung [the alms are collected], the Minister and Assistants bring in the elements and place them on the Communion table; and the Communicants take their places at the table or tables.

Minister.—* The grace of the Lord Jesus Christ, and the love of God, and the fellowship of the Holy Ghost, be with you all.

𝕬𝖒𝖊𝖓.

Minister.—Beloved in the Lord, attend to the words of the Institution of the Holy Supper of our Lord Jesus Christ, as they are delivered by the holy apostle Paul (1 Cor. xi. 23-26) :—" I have received of the Lord that which also I delivered unto you, That the Lord Jesus the same night in which He was betrayed took bread : and when He had given thanks, He brake it, and said, Take, eat : this is my body, which is broken for you : this do in remembrance of me. After the same manner

The Institution. †

---

* The use of the Apostolic Benediction in this place is primitive, and is in accordance with the Reformed practice of beginning all services with a salutation or invocation.

† The use of the Words of Institution here is in accordance with the Directory, which attributes to them an effect in setting apart the elements. The Directory appoints that they are to be given only to the 27th verse, self-examination having been attended to before.

also He took the cup, when He had supped, saying, This cup is the new covenant in my blood : this do ye, as oft as ye drink it, in remembrance of me. For as often as ye eat this bread, and drink this cup, ye do show the Lord's death till He come."

*The Address.** Dearly beloved,—The end for which the Lord hath instituted His Holy Supper is, that "we do this in remembrance of Him;" and after this manner are we to remember him by it.

Setting apart these elements by the Word and prayer to be sacramentally the body and blood of Christ, we must be fully persuaded in our hearts of the mystery of His holy incarnation—God manifest in the flesh ; that He was sent of the Father into the world, and assumed our flesh and blood, as the second Adam, the Lord from heaven.

That having taken our nature, He endured for us the curse and punishment of sin, and thereby satisfied divine justice ; that He was

---

* An Address in this place is in accordance with the Directory. The purpose of it is to show how we are to remember Christ in the Supper. The basis of it is the second part of the Reformed exhortations—viz., the end for which the Supper was instituted ; the first part referring to the persons who should communicate. We have followed more particularly the Dutch liturgy, which has the four leading ideas here given. The wording is a compilation.

bound that we might be set free; was reviled that we might come to honour; was condemned that we might be acquitted at the judgment-seat of God; yea, that He suffered His blessed body to be nailed to the cross, and bowed His head in death, that we might be accepted of God and raised to life in him;—and this one offering up of Himself once for all we are to commemorate and show forth in the breaking of bread, with a spiritual oblation of all possible praise unto God for the same.

And as the Lord hath ordained that we are to eat of this bread, and drink of this cup, to assure us of our union with Him, and that He giveth us His body and His blood to be our meat and our drink unto life eternal, we are not to doubt His goodness, but to be firmly persuaded that He accomplisheth spiritually in us all that He outwardly exhibits. For "the cup of blessing which we bless, is it not the communion of the blood of Christ? the bread which we break, is it not the communion of the body of Christ?"

And as by His death He hath obtained for us the life-giving Spirit, which, dwelling in Him as the Head, and in us as His members, unites us all in one body, we are to receive this Supper in brotherly love, and mindful of the communion of saints. " For we, being many, are one body; for we are all partakers of that one bread." We are to rejoice in the holy fellowship wherein we have part with the faithful patriarchs and prophets of old; the holy apostles and evangelists; the blessed martyrs and confessors; the redeemed of all ages who have died in the Lord, and now live with Him for evermore; our fathers, our brethren, our children, and the friends who were as our own souls: believing that though our eyes behold them no more, they have not perished, but that as "Jesus died and rose again, even so them also which sleep in Jesus will God bring with Him."

And now, that we may fulfil the Saviour's Institution with righteousness and joy, let us draw near to the throne of grace, seeking the increase of our faith and the pardon of our sins, and then, trusting in the divine mercy, let us lift up our hearts, and give thanks unto the Lord our God.

Prayer.

Profession of Faith. ALMIGHTY and eternal God, with Thy holy Church throughout all the world, We believe in Thee, the Father Almighty, Maker of heaven and earth;* and in

---

* The Apostolic Creed is the most catholic, and is given in all the Reformed services. If the second form of the exhortation before Communion be used, the Creed will be omitted here, and the prayer begin with the prayer of access: or the Creed may be introduced *after* the consecration prayer, as in the Dutch liturgy, with this form of words: "Vouchsafe, O Lord, to

Jesus Christ Thine only Son our Lord, who was conceived by the Holy Ghost, born of the Virgin Mary, suffered under Pontius Pilate, was crucified, dead, and buried; He descended into hell; the third day He rose again from the dead; He ascended into heaven, and sitteth on the right hand of God the Father Almighty; from thence He shall come to judge the quick and the dead. We believe in the Holy Ghost; the holy catholic Church; the communion of saints; the forgiveness of sins; the resurrection of the body; and the life everlasting.

Amen.

Lord, increase our faith.

Prayer of Access. ALMIGHTY God, our heavenly Father, who admittest Thy people into such wonderful communion, that partaking of the body and blood of Thy dear Son, they should dwell in Him, and He in them; we unworthy sinners, approaching Thy presence, and beholding Thy glory, do abhor ourselves, and repent in dust and ashes. We have grievously sinned against Thee in thought, in word, and in deed, provoking most justly Thy wrath and indignation against us. We have broken our past

---

strengthen us in the Christian faith, whereof we make our confession; saying, in the communion of the universal Church,. 'I believe,'" &c.

vows, we have dishonoured Thy holy name, and are unworthy of the least of all Thy mercies.

Yet now, most gracious Father, have mercy upon us; for the sake of Jesus Christ forgive us all our sins; purify us from all uncleanness in spirit and in flesh; enable us heartily to forgive others as we beseech Thee to forgive us; and grant that we may hereafter serve Thee in newness of life to the glory of Thy holy name.

O God, who by the blood of Thy dear Son hast consecrated for us a new and living way into the holiest of all, grant unto us, we beseech Thee, the assurance of Thy mercy, and sanctify us by Thy Holy Spirit, that drawing near unto Thee in these holy mysteries with a pure heart and undefiled conscience, we may offer unto Thee a sacrifice in righteousness; through Jesus Christ our Lord.

Amen.

The Eucharistic Prayer. IT is very meet and right, above all things, to give thanks unto Thee, O eternal God: who, by Thy word, didst create heaven and earth, and all things therein: who didst, at the first, make man after Thine own image and likeness, and by whose providence we and all things living are sustained. For all Thy bounties known to us, for all unknown, we give Thee thanks; but chiefly that when, through disobedience, we had fallen from Thee, Thou didst not suffer us to depart from Thee for ever, but hast ransomed us from eternal death, and given us the joyful hope of everlasting life, through Jesus Christ Thy Son; who, being very and eternal God, dwelling with Thee before all time, in glory and blessedness unspeakable, came down from heaven and became Man for us men, and for our salvation.

Not as we ought, but as we are able, we bless Thee for His holy incarnation; for His life on earth; for His precious sufferings and death upon the cross; for His resurrection from the dead; and for His glorious ascension to Thy right hand.

We bless Thee for the giving of the Holy Ghost; for the sacraments and ordinances of the Church; for the communion of Christ's body and blood; for the great hope of everlasting life, and of an eternal weight of glory.

Thee, mighty God, heavenly King, we magnify and praise. With angels and archangels, and all the hosts of heaven, we worship and adore Thy glorious name, joining in the song of cherubim and seraphim, and saying:—

* Holy, Holy, Holy, Lord God of Sabaoth, heaven and earth are full of Thy glory. Hosanna in the highest. Blessed is He that cometh in the name of the Lord. Hosanna in the highest.

* Anciently the people joined aloud in this hymn.

The Invocation.*   AND we most humbly beseech Thee, O merciful Father, to vouchsafe unto us Thy gracious presence, as we now make that memorial of His most blessed sacrifice which Thy Son hath commanded us to make: and to bless and sanctify with Thy Word and Spirit these Thine own gifts of bread and wine which we set before Thee; that we, receiving them, according to our Saviour's institution, in thankful remembrance of His death and passion, may, through the power of the Holy Ghost, be very partakers of His body and blood, with all His benefits, to our salvation and the glory of Thy most holy name.

Amen.

The Lord's Prayer.   OUR Father which art in heaven, Hallowed be Thy name. Thy kingdom come. Thy will be done in earth, as it is in heaven. Give us this day our daily bread. And forgive us our debts, as we forgive our debtors. And lead us not into temptation, but deliver us from evil: for Thine is the kingdom, and the power, and the glory, for ever.

Amen.

---

* This consecrating prayer is in accordance with ancient forms, and with the Directory. The form here given is a compilation from various services.

The Communion.*

Minister.—According to the institution, example, and command of OUR LORD JESUS CHRIST, and in remembrance of Him, we do this—WHO, THE SAME NIGHT IN WHICH HE WAS BETRAYED, TOOK BREAD [*here he shall take some of the bread into his hands*], AND WHEN HE HAD GIVEN THANKS HE BRAKE IT [*here he shall break the bread*] AND SAID, TAKE, EAT, THIS IS MY BODY WHICH IS BROKEN FOR YOU : THIS DO IN REMEMBRANCE OF ME [*here he shall distribute the bread to the assistants, and shall himself partake. Then he shall say—*]
AFTER THE SAME MANNER, ALSO, HE TOOK THE CUP [*here he shall take the cup into his hand*], WHEN HE HAD SUPPED, SAYING, THIS CUP IS THE NEW TESTAMENT IN MY BLOOD : THIS DO YE, AS OFT AS YE DRINK IT, IN REMEMBRANCE OF ME. [*Here the cup is to be given.*]
When one and all have received, the Minister shall say—]† The peace of the Lord Jesus Christ be with you all.
‡ *If there be more than can be accommodated at*

---

* The Neufchatel service has—"Receive our prayers and praises, O merciful God, which we present unto Thee by Jesus Christ—who, the same night," &c.

† These words were of old always addressed to the communicants when at the table.

‡ These directions are in accordance with the Reformed ritu-

one time, the first company of Communicants then withdraw, singing the ciii. Psalm, and others take their places—and the service is renewed as before, till all have communicated. At all tables after the first, the Minister shall begin at the words, " Take, eat," &c.

Exhortation to Thankfulness.* Beloved in the Lord, since the Lord hath now fed our souls at His table, let us praise His holy name with thanksgiving, who hath not spared His own Son, but delivered Him for us all, and given us all things with Him: who commendeth His love toward us in that, while we were yet sinners, Christ died for us; much more then being now justified by His blood, we shall be saved from wrath through Him. For if, when we were enemies, we were reconciled to God by

als. They make no provision for table addresses. It was never intended that such addresses should extend beyond a sentence or two. A very interesting arrangement for Communion is to be seen in the old French Church of A'Lasco in London, where there is a chancel, and a long permanent Communion table within rails, forward from the wall. At Communion the minister takes his place behind, and the people take their seats at the table in companies of about twenty-five, receive, and make room for others.

At the same time, the practice of simultaneous Communion in pews or otherwise presents many advantages.

* According to our service, a few words of address are necessary here. The Dutch liturgy has some verses of thanksgiving in this place, and from it the above is taken. It is not so much an address as a call to thanksgiving and to thankful living.

the death of His Son; much more, being reconciled, we shall be saved by His life. Let us, therefore, show forth His praise from this time forth for evermore, glorifying God in our bodies and in our spirits, which are His; ever walking worthy of His grace, and of our high calling in Christ Jesus.

Let us Pray.

Prayer of Thanks and Self-Dedication. ALMIGHTY and everlasting God, we most heartily thank Thee that Thou hast now vouchsafed to feed us with the spiritual food of the most precious body and blood of Thy Son our Saviour Jesus Christ, assuring us thereby that we are very members incorporate in the mystical body of Thy Son, and heirs through hope of Thine everlasting kingdom. And we beseech Thee, O heavenly Father, so to assist us with Thy grace that we may continue in that holy fellowship, and do all such good works as Thou hast before ordained that we should walk in them; through Jesus Christ our Lord.

We offer and present ourselves unto Thee, our souls and our bodies, and dedicate ourselves wholly to Thy service, henceforth to live only to Thy glory. Thou art our God, and we will praise Thee: Thou art our God, we will exalt Thee.

Interces-sion for the Church militant. O GOD, the Father of our Lord Jesus Christ, of whom the whole family in heaven and in earth is named, we desire at this time, gathered around Thy holy table, to remember before Thee all with whom we have part in the communion of Thy saints.

Look down in mercy, we beseech Thee, on Thy Church militant here upon earth.

Give grace, O heavenly Father, unto all who bear office in Thy Church, that they may fulfil their several ministries in Thy fear, and in purity of heart; and to all Thy people, that they may be holy and obedient, and may come behind in no gift, waiting for the coming of our Lord Jesus Christ.

Especially we commend unto Thee the Pastor of this parish, and people therein, beseeching Thee to accept and increase their piety and faith.

O merciful God, look down upon Thy desolate heritage, upon Thy scattered and divided people. Put away all schisms and heresies from among them; cleanse Thy sanctuary from all defilement of superstition, will-worship, and infidelity; and grant unto all that seek Thee the joy and comfort of the Holy Ghost, and unto Thy whole Church unity and peace.

We pray for all estates of men in Christian lands; for kings, princes, and governors; for nobles and men of estate, and for all the people; and we beseech Thee so to dispose the affairs of all nations that righteousness and truth may prevail, and that we may lead quiet and peaceable lives in all godliness and honesty. Especially we pray for our country; for Thy servant her most sacred Majesty Queen Victoria, for Albert Edward Prince of Wales, the Princess of Wales, and all the Royal Family.

Send forth the news of Thy salvation unto the ends of the earth, and turn the hearts of men everywhere, that they may become obedient to the faith.

Vouchsafe unto us seasonable weather; give and preserve to our use the fruits of the earth, and save us from war, pestilence, and famine.

Comfort and succour, we beseech Thee, all Thy people who are in trouble, sorrow, need, sickness, or any other adversity.

And especially we commend unto Thee those departing this life: be present to them, in Thy mercy and Thy love, in that last hour when heart and flesh do fail; defend them against the assaults of the devil, and give them such patient hope and confidence, that they may joyfully commit their spirits to Thy hands, and do Thou receive them to Thy rest.

Thanks for the Church triumphant. AND rejoicing in the communion of Thy saints, we bless Thy holy name for all Thy servants who have departed in the faith, and who, having accomplished their warfare, are at rest with Thee; beseeching Thee to enable us so to follow their faith and good example, that we with them may finally be partakers of Thy heavenly kingdom—when, made like unto Christ, we shall behold Him with unveiled face, rejoicing in His glory, and by Him we, with all Thy Church, holy and unspotted, shall be presented with exceeding joy before the presence of Thy glory. Hear us, O heavenly Father, for His sake: to whom, with Thee and the Holy Ghost, be glory for ever and ever.

Amen.

Then may be sung the Song of Simeon.

THE BENEDICTION.

NOW the God of peace, that brought again from the dead our Lord Jesus, that great Shepherd of the sheep, through the blood of the everlasting covenant, make you perfect in every good work to do His will, working in you that which is well-pleasing in His sight, through Jesus Christ; to whom be glory for ever and ever.

Amen.

The Solemnization of Matrimony.

I.

Marriage Service.

The persons to be married being present, with a sufficient number of witnesses, the man standing on the right hand and the woman on the left*—

The Minister shall say:

OUR help is in the name of the Lord, who made heaven and earth.

Dearly beloved,—We are here assembled before God to join this man, A. B., and this woman, C. D., in holy matrimony. If any person can show just cause why they may not be lawfully joined together, let him now speak, or else, hereafter, for ever hold his peace.

* The service ought to be held "in the place appointed by authority for public worship."—Directory.

Then speaking to the persons that are to be married, he shall say:

I require and charge you both, as ye will answer at the day of judgment, when the secrets of all hearts shall be disclosed, that if either of you know any impediment why ye may not be lawfully joined together in matrimony, ye do now confess it. For be ye well assured that so many as are coupled together otherwise than God's Word doth allow, are not joined together by God; neither is their matrimony lawful.

If no impediment be alleged or confessed, the Minister shall offer one or other of the prayers that follow.

Let us Pray.

ALMIGHTY and most merciful Father, we Thy sinful and unworthy children praise Thee for all the gifts of Thy providence, and for all the bounties of Thy grace. Especially do we at this time thank Thee for the institution of marriage, and that Thou hast made it to be honourable in all. And we humbly beseech Thee graciously to bless these Thy servants who are about to be joined together in matrimony, according to Thine own ordinance. Sanctify them by Thy Spirit, giving them a new frame of mind fit for their new estate. Enrich them

THE SOLEMNIZATION OF MATRIMONY. 243

with all grace, whereby they may perform the duties, enjoy the comforts, sustain the cares, and resist the temptations of that estate, as becometh Christians. May they, being united to each other in the marriage covenant, be united unto Thee in that covenant which is ordered in all things and sure; through Jesus Christ our Lord.

Amen.

Or,

ALMIGHTY God, our heavenly Father, from whom cometh down every good and perfect gift; lift Thou the light of Thy countenance, we beseech Thee, upon us, Thine unworthy servants. May Thy blessing, which maketh rich and addeth no sorrow, rest upon Thy servants who are now about to be united in holy matrimony according to Thine own institution and ordinance. Grant that, acknowledging Thee and seeking to please Thee in this and in all things, they may be made exceeding glad with Thy countenance, and may enjoy Thy loving-kindness which is better than life; through Jesus Christ our Lord.

Amen.

Then the Minister may exhort the man and woman after this manner:

Marriage is a holy and honourable estate instituted by God, and sanctified by the presence and first miracle of Christ, at the wedding-feast in Cana of Galilee; commended in Holy Scripture as honourable in all; and consecrated as signifying the union and mutual love of Christ and His Church. It is therefore not to be entered upon lightly nor unadvisedly, but thoughtfully, soberly, and in the fear of God, with due consideration of the purposes for which it was ordained, and the duties which it imposes. And that you may rightly understand and duly perform these, you must give heed to the counsels of God, recorded for your instruction in His holy Word; for thus only can you hope together to fulfil His will and inherit His blessing.

It is written in the Epistle of S. Paul to the Ephesians, in the 5th chapter, at the 22d verse: " Wives, submit yourselves unto your own husbands, as unto the Lord. For the husband is the head of the wife, even as Christ is the Head of the Church: and He is the saviour of the body. Therefore as the Church is subject unto Christ, so let the wives be to their own husbands in everything. Husbands, love your wives, even as Christ also loved the Church, and gave Himself for it; that He might sanctify and cleanse it with the washing of water by the word, that He might present it to Himself a glorious Church, not having spot, or wrinkle, or any such thing; but that it should be holy and without blemish. So ought men to love their wives as their own bodies. He that loveth his wife loveth himself. For no man ever yet hated his own flesh, but nourisheth and cherisheth it, even as the Lord the Church: for we are members of His body, of His flesh, and of His bones. For this cause shall a man leave his father and mother, and shall be joined unto his wife, and they two shall be one flesh. This is a great mystery: but I speak concerning Christ and the Church. Nevertheless let every one of you in particular so love his wife even as himself; and the wife see that she reverence her husband."

Or,

God created man in His own image, and said, It is not good that the man should be alone: I will make him an help meet for him; and He brought unto the man the woman whom He had made. And Adam said, This is now bone of my bones, and flesh of my flesh. Therefore shall a man leave father and mother, and cleave unto his wife: and they twain shall be one flesh.

Marriage, thus ordained of God in Eden, was confirmed at the wedding in Cana of Galilee by the gracious presence and miraculous blessing of the Lord Jesus Christ : who also hath said, What God hath joined together, let not man put asunder. Moreover, His holy apostle Paul hath commended unto the husband the example of Christ in loving His Church, and unto the wife the willing subjection of the Church unto Christ as her Head ; teaching us that marriage is well-pleasing to God our Saviour, and honourable to all who maintain therein a mutual love and unshaken fidelity.

It is written in the 1st Epistle of S. Peter, in the 3d chapter, at the 1st verse : " Likewise, ye wives, be in subjection to your own husbands ; that if any obey not the word, they also may without the word be won by the conversation of the wives ; while they behold your chaste conversation coupled with fear. Whose adorning let it not be that outward adorning of plaiting the hair, and of wearing of gold, or of putting on of apparel ; but let it be the hidden man of the heart, in that which is not corruptible, even the ornament of a meek and quiet spirit, which is in the sight of God of great price. For after this manner in the old time the holy women also, who trusted in God, adorned themselves, being in subjection unto their own husbands ;

even as Sara obeyed Abraham, calling him lord: whose daughters ye are as long as ye do well, and are not afraid with any amazement. Likewise, ye husbands, dwell with them according to knowledge, giving honour unto the wife, as unto the weaker vessel, and as being heirs together of the grace of life; that your prayers be not hindered."

Then the Minister shall say:

To these, and the other instructions of God's Word, I charge you both ever to give heed, seeking earnestly His help and grace, that so your union may be fruitful of comfort in this life, and a furtherance of your soul's salvation, to the glory of His holy name.

As a seal to the vow which you are about to take, take each other by the right hand.

The Minister shall then cause the man, holding the woman by the right hand, to repeat these words:

I, *A.*, do take thee, *C.*, to be my wedded wife; and do, in the presence of God and before this congregation, promise and covenant to be a loving and faithful husband unto thee, until God shall separate us by death.

Then the woman, holding the man by the right hand, shall say:

I, *C.*, do take thee, *A.*, to be my wedded husband; and do, in the presence of God and before this congregation, promise and covenant to be a loving, faithful, and obedient wife unto thee, until God shall separate us by death.

[*When a ring is used, the Minister shall say:*

This ring is given and received in token of fidelity to these vows.

Then the man, the Minister guiding his hand, shall place the ring on the fourth finger of her left hand.]

Then the Minister shall say:

Forasmuch as you have covenanted together in holy wedlock, and have declared the same before God and these witnesses, I, in the name of God, whose minister I am, pronounce you married, husband and wife. Whom God hath joined together let not man put asunder.

The Lord bless you and keep you. The Lord make His face to shine upon you, and be gracious unto you. The Lord lift up His countenance upon you, and give you peace.

Amen.

Let us pray.

ALMIGHTY God, who showest Thy wisdom and goodness in all Thine ordinances and works; who hast said from the beginning that it is not good that man should be alone, and for that cause madest a help meet for him, ordaining that these twain should be one flesh; we beseech Thee to give Thy Holy Spirit to these two persons whom Thou hast called to the holy estate of marriage; that they may live together in all purity and faith according to Thy will. Bless them, O Lord, as Thou blessedst those faithful fathers, Thy friends and servants, Abraham, Isaac, and Jacob; make them partakers of that covenant which Thou didst confirm to those Thy servants, that having holy lineage, they may bring them up to Thy praise and glory. Hear us, Father of all mercies, through Jesus Christ our Lord.
Amen.

Or,

O GOD most holy, Creator of all things, who didst bless the first man and woman, saying, Increase and multiply and replenish the earth, and have dominion over it; Thou who didst by the holy union of marriage make both of them one being; Thou who didst bless Thy servants Abraham, Isaac, and Jacob, making them the fathers of many nations; Thou who didst receive the prayers of Zacharias and Elizabeth, and gavest to them the Forerunner for a son: Thou who from the root of Jesse didst produce in the flesh the Virgin Mary, of whom Thy Son was born for the salvation of mankind—He who was present in Cana of Galilee, and blessed the wedding-feast, so as to make it manifest that lawful marriage is according to Thy will; Thou, O Lord most holy, receive our supplications, and be pleased to bless this marriage, and to give to both these Thy servants a quiet life, and to see long days in chastity and love to one another. Bind them together with the tie of peace; give them a lasting posterity; bless them in their children; grant them that crown of glory which never fadeth; enable them to see the sons of their sons; keep their wedded life safe from all evil. Give them of the dew of heaven above, and of the fatness of the earth below; fill their dwelling with corn and wine and oil and all good things, that they may give to the needy of what they possess. And grant unto them and to all present the means of salvation. For Thou art a merciful God and a lover of mankind, and to Thee we render the glory, to the Father, to the Son, and to the Holy Spirit, world without end.

Amen.

THE SOLEMNIZATION OF MATRIMONY. 251

Or,

O GOD, the author and giver of all good things, who hast consecrated this estate of marriage, and made it holy, by Thine own institution and blessing, and by the mystery whereby it sets forth the union of all faithful souls with Jesus Christ, our great Husband and Head, Let Thy blessing, we humbly entreat thee, descend and rest upon these Thy servants, who have now been joined together. Grant unto them health, prosperity, and peace. May they dwell together in unity and love all the days of their life. And, above all things, O Lord, we pray Thee to enrich their souls with Thy heavenly grace, that they may obey and serve Thee all their days, walking in the steps of Jesus Christ Thy Son, and adorning His doctrine; that, finally, when the joys and sorrows, and all the good and evil of this transitory world are ended, they may inherit Thy promises, and be made partakers of eternal joy in the kingdom of heaven; where they neither marry nor are given in marriage, but are as the angels of God.

O Lord Almighty, who dost invite us all, in Thy Gospel, to the great marriage-supper of Thy Son, So incline our hearts by Thy good Spirit, that we may yield obedience to Thy gracious call and come to the wedding; and may we, each one, be so clothed in the garments of righteousness and true holiness, that we may be accepted of Thee, and may sit down with Abraham, and Isaac, and Jacob, and all Thy saints, to enjoy for ever that banquet of unutterable felicity which Thou hast prepared for them that love Thee.

O Thou, whose only Son, Jesus Christ, did first display His divine power by turning water into wine at that marriage in Cana which He beautified with His presence, Turn, we pray Thee, the water into wine, to us Thy servants; that all our temporal mercies being sanctified to us, may become spiritual blessings, and means of life and salvation; through Jesus Christ our Redeemer.

Amen.

OUR Father which art in heaven, Hallowed be Thy name. Thy kingdom come. Thy will be done in earth, as it is in heaven. Give us this day our daily bread. And forgive us our debts, as we forgive our debtors. And lead us not into temptation; but deliver us from evil.

Amen.

If it be convenient, the 67th or the 128th Psalm may be here sung.

THE grace of the Lord Jesus Christ, and the love of God, and the communion of the Holy Ghost, be with you all.
Amen.

Manual for the Burial of the Dead.

On no occasion does the recognition, by solemn acts of worship, of the relation in which we stand to God, seem more appropriate, or more likely to be profitable, than when the living are called by His providence to commit the remains of their brethren to the grave. And although the errors springing from the doctrine of Purgatory led the Fathers of the Reformation in Scotland to discountenance all religious observances at interments, the venerable relic entitled "The Forme and Manner of Buriall usit in the Kirk of Montrois," preserved in Vol. I. of the Wodrow Miscellany, shows that even in their own day their views were not everywhere adopted or enforced. The gradual and general resumption of prayer at funerals has long since proclaimed the universal conviction that no good reason for omitting on such occasions the devotional observances solemnizing and comforting to the living can be found in the fact of their having once been regarded as beneficial to the dead.

But while nothing needs to be said in favour of a practice which is universal amongst us, two peculiarities in the usage of Scottish Presbyterians call for remark.

1. In many, if not most, parts of the country, the religious observance at present consists of prayer alone; while the special means of grace which of all others seems on such occasions the best fitted at once to impress the thoughtless and to comfort the mourning, as well as to guard against error—the solemn reading of the pure Word of God, without which no Protestant Service is true to its character, or complete—is generally omitted. Man speaks to God, but God, though calling and disposing man by His providence to listen, is not allowed to speak plainly to man in His own word.

2. The religious Service at funerals in Scotland is, as a general rule, confined to the house of mourning, except on the occasion of the death of ministers, and of others who have filled positions of special prominence, when sometimes a

Service is held at the Church or the place of interment. Yet it must be admitted that circumstances frequently occur in which it is impracticable or inexpedient that the persons assembled should be collected into the house. For such cases, at least, it is desirable that some Service of a public kind should be provided.

Nor should it be forgotten, as it appears too generally to be, that the Scottish Church is no longer, as she was even thirty years ago, all but confined to the mother country, but has spread and is spreading herself in all parts of the world; and that a provincial singularity of usage, little injurious within her former territorial limits, may very greatly impede her usefulness to multitudes, originally belonging to other British and Continental communions, who are willing to accept her pure ministrations, and to place themselves under her wholesome teaching, but who are repelled from permanent and full connection with her by peculiarities repugnant to their feelings and habits, and in the maintenance of which no religious principle is involved.

In some parts of the world a Service at the place of interment already is, and has long been, held by the ministers of the Church of Scotland, in conformity with the feelings and usage of other Evangelical denominations ; and in some places abroad, such a Service is in fact indispensable, the register and certificate of the clergyman officiating at the cemetery being there the ordinary legal evidence of decease. Surely it is desirable that some common directory should be provided for such circumstances as these.

The following draft contains, first, a Service for use at the house, or rather a Manual of suitable portions of Scripture collected and arranged for the convenience of the conductor of the Service,* with forms of prayer (the latter of which is from the Dutch Reformed Liturgy); and, secondly, a scheme of Service to be used in public, of which it is intended that such parts should be used, and at such time and place, as may seem expedient.

In respect to the public portion of the Service —while the aim of the Society is rather to bring into notice the devotional materials already

* Taken, with some change and addition, from the Manual of Devotional Services recommended by the most influential Bishops and Ministers of the orthodox Churches in the United States, and in general use in that country.

sanctioned by use in various branches of the Church, than to originate new forms—it could not be overlooked that here the ground has long been preoccupied, as regards the vast majority of the English-speaking portion of mankind, by a Service of which, notwithstanding one or two blemishes easily removed, the excellence is universally admitted; which has the inestimable merit of consisting, to the extent of above three-fourths, of pure Scripture; and which for many generations, in all regions of the world, has been endeared to British and American Protestants of almost every ecclesiastical connection, as the common expression of Christian sorrow, resignation, and hope, in the sight of death and the grave.

There may be in some minds a strange pride or vanity which would see in the use of a formula by others a reason rather against than in favour of its adoption. Such feelings, if comprehensible at all, seem utterly incapable of rational defence; and it is believed that to the great majority of Christians it will be the highest possible recommendation of that which is in itself good, or easily made so, that it should bring those who differ in other respects and at other times into visible unity as brethren there, where surely all differences ought to disappear. The attempt to introduce a totally new Burial Service into the English language at the present day would be, in the great interests of Christian charity, a retrograde step.

In this view, the portion of this Service designed for public use has been so framed as to present the English Burial Service nearly entire, with the few short alterations desired by the Presbyterians of England at the Savoy Conference, and in the form in which substantially it is used by many Christians of various denominations in America. At the same time, the variety and liberty awanting in that Service have been provided for by introducing, in addition to the Scripture passages that form part of it, several others proper for such occasions. The only addition, except from Scripture, is the beautifully comprehensive prayer of Jeremy Taylor; but the plan admits of the introduction of any other suitable prayers.

Service at the Burial of the Dead.

I.—AT THE HOUSE.

LET us hear the Word of God written for our admonition and comfort.

After one or more of these introductory verses may be read one of the Collections of Scripture sentences following them.

It is better to go to the house of mourning than to go to the house of feasting, for that is the end of all men, and the living will lay it to his heart.—Eccl. vii. 2.

Affliction cometh not forth of the dust, neither doth trouble spring out of the ground. See now, saith the Lord, that I, even I am he, and there is no God with me. I kill, and I make alive; I wound, and I heal; neither is there any that can deliver out of my hand.—Job v. 6; Deut. xxxii. 39.

Lord, make me to know mine end, and the measure of my days, what it is; that I may know how frail I am. For I know that Thou wilt bring me to death, and to the house appointed for all living. — Ps. xxxix. 4; Job xxx. 23.

For Admonition of the Living.

I.

What man is he that liveth, and shall not see death? Shall he deliver his soul from the hand of the grave? One dieth in his full strength, being wholly at ease and quiet; another dieth in the bitterness of his soul, and never eateth with pleasure: they shall lie down alike in the dust, and the worms shall cover them. All flesh shall perish together, and man shall turn again into dust.—Ps. lxxxix. 48; Job xxi. 23, 25, 26, xxxii. 15.

There is hope of a tree, if it be cut down, that it will sprout again, and that the tender branch thereof will not cease. Though the root thereof wax old in the earth, and the stock thereof die in the ground; yet through the scent of water it will bring forth boughs like a plant. But man dieth, and wasteth away; yea, man giveth up the ghost, and where is he? As the waters fail from the sea, and the flood decayeth and drieth up:

so man lieth down, and riseth not: till the heavens be no more they shall not awake, nor be raised out of their sleep.—Job xiv. 7-12.

If a man die, shall he live again? Jesus said unto Martha, I am the resurrection and the life: he that believeth in me, though he were dead, yet shall he live. And whosoever liveth and believeth in me shall never die.—Job xiv. 14; John xi. 25, 26.

It is appointed unto men once to die, but after this the judgment. We must all appear before the judgment-seat of Christ, that every one may receive the things done in his body, according to that he hath done, whether it be good or bad. If the tree fall toward the south or toward the north; in the place where the tree falleth, there it shall be. He that is unjust, let him be unjust still; and he that is filthy, let him be filthy still; and he that is righteous, let him be righteous still; and he that is holy, let him be holy still. And behold, saith the Lord, I come quickly, and my reward is with me, to give every man according as his work shall be.—Heb. ix. 27; 2 Cor. v. 10; Eccl. xi. 3; Rev. xxii. 11, 12.

The righteous hath hope in his death. Let me die the death of the righteous, and let my last end be like his. Precious in the sight of the Lord is the death of His saints. They shall hunger no more, neither thirst any more; neither shall the sun light on them, nor any heat. And there shall be no more death, neither sorrow nor crying, neither shall there be any more pain: for the former things are passed away. And God shall wipe away all tears from their eyes.—Prov. xiv. 32; Num. xxiii. 10; Ps. cxvi. 15; Rev. vii. 16, xxi. 4, vii. 17.

II.

Man is like to vanity: his days are as a shadow that passeth away. His breath goeth forth, he returneth to his earth; in that very day his thoughts perish.—Ps. cxliv. 4, cxlvi. 4.

When he dieth he shall carry nothing away; his glory shall not descend after him. As he came forth from his mother's womb, naked shall he return to go as he came, and he shall take nothing of his labour which he may carry away in his hand. We brought nothing into this world, and it is certain we can carry nothing out. —Ps. xlix. 17; Eccl. v. 15; 1 Tim. vi. 7.

What is your life? It is even a vapour which appeareth for a little time, and then vanisheth away. Our days on earth are as a shadow, and there is none abiding. We spend our years as a tale that is told. The days of our years are threescore years and ten; and if, by reason of strength, they be fourscore years, yet is their strength labour and sorrow, for it is soon cut off, and we fly away. We all do fade as a leaf, and our iniquities like the wind have taken us away. —James iv. 14 ; 1 Chron. xxix. 15 ; Ps. xc. 9, 10 ; Isa. lxiv. 6.

Boast not thyself of to-morrow, for thou knowest not what a day may bring forth. For man also knoweth not his time ; as the fishes that are taken in an evil net, and as the birds that are caught in the snare, so are the sons of men snared in an evil time, when it falleth suddenly upon them. O my God, take me not away in the midst of my days, for I am a stranger with Thee, and a sojourner, as all my fathers were. O spare me, that I may recover strength, before I go hence, and be no more.—Prov. xxvii. 1 ; Eccl. ix. 12 ; Ps. cii. 24, xxxix. 12, 13.

Brethren, the time is short ; it remaineth that they that weep be as though they wept not ; and they that rejoice, as though they rejoiced not ; and they that buy, as though they possessed not ; and they that use this world as not abusing it : for the fashion of this world passeth away.— 1 Cor. vii. 29, 30, 31.

The night cometh when no man can work. Whatsoever thy hand findeth to do, do it with thy might ; for there is no work, nor device, nor wisdom, nor knowledge, in the grave, whither thou goest. Seek ye the Lord while He may be found, call ye upon Him while He is near; let the wicked forsake his way, and the unrighteous man his thoughts ; and let him return unto the Lord, and He will have mercy upon him; and to our God, for He will abundantly pardon. The wages of sin is death, but the gift of God is eternal life through Jesus Christ our Lord. —John ix. 4; Eccl. ix. 10; Isa. lv. 6, 7; Rom. vi. 23.

For Consolation of the Bereaved.

I.

Thou shalt forget thy misery, and remember it as waters that pass away. Weeping may endure for a night, but joy cometh in the morning. Cast thy burden upon the Lord, and He shall sustain thee. He hath not despised nor abhorred the affliction of the afflicted; neither hath He hid His face from him; but when he cried unto Him, He heard. Though He cause grief, yet will He have compassion according to the multitude of His mercies. For He doth not afflict willingly, nor grieve the children of men.—Job xv. 16; Ps. xxx. 5, lv. 22; Lam. iii. 32, 33.

Despise not thou the chastening of the Lord, nor faint when thou art rebuked of Him: for whom the Lord loveth He chasteneth, and scourgeth every son whom He receiveth. If ye endure chastening, God dealeth with you as with sons; for what son is he whom his father chasteneth not? But if ye be without chastisement, whereof all are partakers, then are ye bastards, and not sons. Furthermore, we have had fathers of our flesh which corrected us, and we gave them reverence: shall we not much rather be in subjection unto the Father of Spirits, and live? For they verily for a few days chastened us after their own pleasure; but He for our profit, that we might be partakers of His holiness. Now, no chastening for the present seemeth joyous, but grievous; nevertheless afterward it yieldeth the peaceable fruit of righteousness unto them which are exercised thereby. Wherefore, lift up the hands which hang down, and the feeble knees. The sufferings of this present time are not worthy to be compared with the glory which shall be revealed in us.—Heb. xii. 5-13; Rom. viii. 18.

God hath comforted His people, and will have mercy on His afflicted. Blessed be God, even the Father of our Lord Jesus Christ, the Father of mercies and the God of all comfort, who comforteth us in all our tribulation, that we may be able to comfort them which are in any trouble, by the comfort wherewith we ourselves are comforted of God. He shall deliver thee in six troubles, yea, in seven there shall no evil touch thee. Wait on the Lord; be of good courage, and He shall strengthen thine heart; wait, I say, on the Lord. — Isa. xlix. 13; 2 Cor. i. 3, 4; Job v. 19; Ps. xxvii. 14.

II.

Shall we receive good at the hand of the Lord, and shall we not receive evil? Behold, happy is the man whom God correcteth; therefore despise not thou the chastening of the Almighty; for He maketh sore, and bindeth up; He woundeth, and His hands make whole.—Job ii. 10, v. 17, 18.

Will the Lord cast off for ever? and will He be favourable no more? Is His mercy clean gone for ever? doth His promise fail for evermore? Hath God forgotten to be gracious? hath He in anger shut up His tender mercies?—Ps. lxxvii. 7, 8, 9.

The Lord will not cast off for ever. For His merciful kindness is great toward us, and the truth of the Lord endureth for ever. The Lord is merciful and gracious, slow to anger, and plenteous in mercy. He will not always chide; neither will He keep His anger for ever. He hath not dealt with us after our sins; nor rewarded us according to our iniquities: for as the heaven is high above the earth, so great is His mercy toward them that fear Him. As far as the east is from the west, so far hath He removed our transgressions from us. Like as a father pitieth his children, so the Lord pitieth them that fear Him; for He knoweth our frame, He remembereth that we are dust. The mercy of the Lord is from everlasting to everlasting upon them that fear Him, and His righteousness unto children's children; to such as keep His covenant, and to those that remember His commandments to do them. A father of the fatherless, and a judge of the widows, is God in His holy habitation. Leave thy fatherless children, saith the Lord, I will preserve them alive; and let thy widows trust in me.—Lam. iii. 31 ; Ps. ciii. 8-18, lxviii. 5 ; Jer. xlix. 11.

When thou art in tribulation, if thou turn to the Lord thy God, and shalt be obedient unto His voice, the Lord thy God is a merciful God ; He will not forsake thee, nor destroy thee. And thou shalt remember all the way which the Lord thy God led thee, to humble thee, and to prove thee, to know what was in thine heart, whether thou wouldest keep His commandments or no. Thou shalt also consider, that as a man chasteneth his son, so the Lord thy God chasteneth thee. That the trial of your faith being much more precious than of gold that perisheth, though it be tried with fire, might be found unto praise, and honour, and glory, at the appearing of Jesus Christ.—Deut. iv. 30, 31, viii. 2, 5 ; 1 Peter i. 7.

III.

Let not your heart be troubled : ye believe in God, believe also in me. In my Father's house are many mansions: if it were not so, I would have told you. I go to prepare a place for you. And if I go and prepare a place for you, I will come again, and receive you unto myself; that where I am, there ye may be also.—John xiv. 1, 2, 3.

I would not have you to be ignorant, brethren, concerning them which are asleep, that ye sorrow not, even as others which have no hope. For if we believe that Jesus died, and rose again, even so them also which sleep in Jesus will God bring with Him. Fear not, saith the Lord, I am the first and the last; I am He that liveth, and was dead; and, behold, I am alive for evermore, Amen; and have the keys of hell and of death. —1 Thess. iv. 13, 14; Rev. i. 17, 18.

Wherefore, seeing we also are compassed about with so great a cloud of witnesses, let us lay aside every weight, and the sin which doth so easily beset us, and let us run with patience the race that is set before us; looking unto Jesus, the author and finisher of our faith; who, for the joy that was set before Him, endured the cross, despising the shame, and is set down at the right hand of the throne of God.—Heb. xii. 1, 2.

IV.

AT THE DEATH OR BURIAL OF A CHILD.

And the Lord struck the child that Uriah's wife bare unto David, and it was very sick. David therefore besought God for the child; and David fasted, and went in, and lay all night upon the earth. And the elders of his house arose, and went to him, to raise him up from the earth: but he would not, neither did he eat bread with them. And it came to pass on the seventh day, that the child died. And the servants of David feared to tell him that the child was dead: for they said, Behold, while the child was yet alive, we spake unto him, and he would not hearken unto our voice: how will he then vex himself, if we tell him that the child is dead? But when David saw that his servants whispered, David perceived that the child was dead: therefore David said unto his servants, Is the child dead? And they said, He is dead. Then David arose from the earth, and washed, and anointed himself, and changed his apparel, and came into the house of the Lord, and worshipped: then he came to his own house; and when he required, they set bread before him, and he did eat. Then said his servants unto him, What thing is this that thou hast done? Thou didst fast and weep for the child, while it was alive; but when the child was dead, thou didst rise and eat bread. And he said, While the child was yet alive, I fasted and wept: for I said, Who can tell whether God will be gracious to me, that the child may live? But now he is dead, wherefore should I fast? can I bring him back again. I shall go to him, but he shall not return to me.—2 Sam. xii. 15-23.

Jesus said, Suffer little children, and forbid them not, to come unto me: for of such is the kingdom of heaven. It is not the will of your Father which is in heaven that one of these little ones should perish. For I say unto you, That in heaven their angels do always behold the face of my Father which is in heaven.—Matt. xix. 14, xviii. 14, 10.

O Lord, our Lord, how excellent is Thy name in all the earth! Out of the mouth of babes and sucklings Thou hast perfected praise. I thank Thee, O Father, Lord of heaven and earth, because Thou hast hid these things from the wise and prudent, and hast revealed them unto babes: even so, Father, for so it seemed good in Thy sight.—Ps. viii. 1, 2; Luke x. 21.

We have not an High Priest which cannot be touched with the feeling of our infirmities; but was in all points tempted like as we are, yet without sin. Let us therefore come boldly unto the throne of grace, that we may obtain mercy, and find grace to help in time of need.—Heb. iv. 15, 16.

The Lord gave, and the Lord hath taken away: blessed be the name of the Lord.—Job i. 21.

Then may follow one of these Prayers, or any other suitable to the occasion.

I.

ETERNAL and ever-blessed God, supreme Disposer of events, out of the depths of our sin and sorrow, we, the frail children of the dust, would lift up our souls unto Thee.

Through all time and change Thou art the same; irresistible in might, yet infinite in wisdom, love, and mercy; our refuge and our strength; our hope, and help, and comfort; our God and Father in Christ.

Clouds and thick darkness are round about Thee, but justice and judgment are the habitation of Thy throne: mercy and truth go before Thy face. Though Thou slay us, yet will we trust in Thee. Our flesh and our heart fail; but Thou art the strength of our heart, and our portion for ever.

Blessed be Thy name, O God, that in Thine unspeakable love Thou didst send Thy wellbeloved Son into this world of sin and death to be our Saviour, that even as sin had reigned unto death, so grace might reign through righteousness unto eternal life, through Jesus Christ our Lord.

Father of mercies and God of all comfort, who dost not afflict willingly the children of men, but lovest those whom Thou chastenest, draw near, we earnestly beseech Thee, with Thine own abundant consolations, to those who are sorrowing for the dead, so that while they mourn, they may not murmur, or faint under Thy rod; but, remembering Thy unnumbered past and present mercies, Thy promises, and all Thy love in Christ, may resign themselves meekly into Thy hands, to be taught and disciplined by Thee. Thou, Lord, knowest their condition, their sorrows, and the secrets of their hearts. Pour into their wounded spirits the balm of Thy fatherly wisdom and compassion; and grant that, loosened from earthly ties, they may cleave the more closely to Thee, who bringest life out of death, and who canst turn their grief into eternal joy.

And now, O merciful God, vouchsafe unto us, who are still spared, grace to receive aright the warnings of Thy providence, and the lessons taught us by the life and death of our fellowmen. May every instance of mortality convince us of the evil of sin, and the vanity of earthly things, and lead us unto Him in whom pardon, peace, and life are to be found, so that we may be delivered from both the power of sin and the fear of death. And grant that, whensoever our call shall come, our souls may depart in peace, and our bodies rest in hope to rise in glory, through the might and merits of Jesus Christ our Saviour, for whom, and through whom, we desire, in life and in death, to bless Thy name; and to whom, with Thee and the Holy Ghost, we would ascribe all glory and praise, world without end.

Amen.

II.

O LORD, merciful God, Father of our Lord Jesus Christ; who hath said, Blessed are they that mourn, for they shall be comforted: under the shadow of Thy judgments we come to Thee, and acknowledge Thee to be the Lord alone. Thou hast entered this house with Thy chastenings. O be Thou nigh in Thy tender compassion to these afflicted ones. Bless Thy sorrowing servants with Thine abounding consolations. Convert them wholly to Thyself, and fill their bleeding hearts with Thy love. Make the night of their grief to be light by Thy grace. Deliver us, Thy servants, we pray Thee, from the bondage of our sins, that we may be free from fear of death, and may be ready at Thy coming. Yea, Lord, for Christ's sake, sanctify us by Thy Holy Spirit, that whether we live, we may live unto the Lord, or whether we die, we may die unto the Lord; whether we live or die, may we be the Lord's.

     Amen.

The grace of our Lord Jesus Christ be with us all.

Amen.

II.—SERVICE IN PUBLIC.

Introductory sentences of Scripture, of which one or more may be read.

Man that is born of a woman is of few days and full of trouble. He cometh forth as a flower, and is cut down: he fleeth also as a shadow, and continueth not.—Job xiv. 1, 2.

I am the resurrection and the life, saith the Lord: he that believeth in me, though he were dead, yet shall he live; and whosoever liveth and believeth in me shall never die.—John xi. 25, 26.

I know that my Redeemer liveth, and that He shall stand at the latter day upon the earth: and though after my skin worms destroy this body, yet in my flesh shall I see God; whom I shall see for myself, and mine eyes shall behold, and not another.—Job xix. 25, 26, 27.

We brought nothing into this world, and it is certain we can carry nothing out. The Lord gave, and the Lord hath taken away; blessed be the name of the Lord.—1 Tim. vi. 7; Job i. 21.

All flesh is as grass, and all the glory of man as the flower of grass. The grass withereth, and the flower thereof falleth away; but the word of the Lord endureth for ever.—1 Peter i. 24, 25.

Then may be used one or both of the Psalms following:

Psalm xxxix.

Lord, make me to know mine end, and the measure of my days, what it is; that I may know how frail I am.

Behold, Thou hast made my days as an handbreadth, and mine age is as nothing before Thee: verily every man at his best state is altogether vanity.

Surely every man walketh in a vain show; surely they are disquieted in vain: he heapeth up riches, and knoweth not who shall gather them.

And now, Lord, what wait I for? my hope is in Thee.

Deliver me from all my transgressions; make me not the reproach of the foolish.

I was dumb, I opened not my mouth; because Thou didst it.

Remove Thy stroke away from me: I am consumed by the blow of Thine hand.

When Thou with rebukes dost correct man for iniquity, Thou makest his beauty to consume away like a moth: surely every man is vanity.

Hear my prayer, O Lord, and give ear unto my cry; hold not Thy peace at my tears: for I am a stranger with Thee, and a sojourner, as all my fathers were.

O spare me, that I may recover strength, before I go hence, and be no more.

Psalm xc.

, Lord, Thou hast been our dwelling-place in all generations.

Before the mountains were brought forth, or ever Thou hadst formed the earth and the world, even from everlasting to everlasting, Thou art God.

Thou turnest man to destruction; and sayest, Return, ye children of men.

For a thousand years in Thy sight are but as yesterday when it is past, and as a watch in the night.

Thou carriest them away as with a flood ; they are as a sleep : in the morning they are like grass which groweth up.

In the morning it flourisheth and groweth up ; in the evening it is cut down, and withereth.

For we are consumed by Thine anger, and by Thy wrath are we troubled.

Thou hast set our iniquities before Thee, our secret sins in the light of Thy countenance.

For all our days are passed away in Thy wrath : we spend our years as a tale that is told.

The days of our years are threescore years and ten ; and if by reason of strength they be fourscore years, yet is their strength labour and sorrow : for it is soon cut off, and we fly away.

Who knoweth the power of Thine anger? even according to Thy fear, so is Thy wrath.

So teach us to number our days, that we may apply our hearts unto wisdom.

Then may follow one or more of these Lessons of Scripture:

Let us hear the Word of the Lord, as it is written for our admonition and comfort.

Mark xiii. 33-37.

Take ye heed, watch and pray : for ye know not when the time is. For the Son of man is as a man taking a far journey, who left his house and gave authority to his servants, and to every man his work, and commanded the porter to watch. Watch ye, therefore: for ye know not when the master of the house cometh, at even, or at midnight, or at the cock-crowing, or in the morning: lest coming suddenly, he find you sleeping. And what I say unto you, I say unto all, Watch.

John xi. 21-27.

Then said Martha unto Jesus, Lord, if Thou hadst been here, my brother had not died. But I know, that even now, whatsoever Thou wilt ask of God, God will give it Thee. Jesus saith unto her, Thy brother shall rise again. Martha saith unto Him, I know that he shall rise again in the resurrection at the last day. Jesus said unto her, I am the resurrection and the life : he that believeth in me, though he were dead, yet shall he live ; and whosoever liveth and believeth in me, shall never die. Believest thou this? She saith unto Him, Yea, Lord : I believe that Thou art the Christ, the Son of God, which should come into the world.

Romans v. 12-21.

As by one man sin entered into the world, and death by sin ; and so death passed upon all men, for that all have sinned: (for until the law sin was in the world: but sin is not imputed when there is no law. Nevertheless death reigned from Adam to Moses, even over them that had not sinned after the similitude of Adam's transgression, who is the figure of Him that was to come. But not as the offence, so also is the free gift. For if through the offence of one many be dead; much more the grace of God, and the gift by grace, which is by one man, Jesus Christ, hath abounded unto many. And not as it was by one that sinned, so is the gift: for the judgment was by one to condemnation, but the free gift is of many offences unto justification. For if by one man's offence death reigned by one; much more they which receive abundance of grace, and of the gift of righteousness, shall reign in life by one, Jesus Christ.) Therefore, as by the offence of one judgment came upon all men to condemnation; even so by the righteousness of one the free gift came upon all men unto justification of life. For as by one man's disobedience many were made sinners; so by the obedience of one shall many be made righteous. Moreover, the law entered, that the offence might abound: but where sin abounded, grace did much more abound: that as sin hath reigned unto death, even so might grace reign through righteousness unto eternal life by Jesus Christ our Lord.

1 *Corinthians* xv. 20-58.

Now is Christ risen from the dead, and become the first-fruits of them that slept. For since by man came death, by man came also the resurrection of the dead. For as in Adam all die, even so in Christ shall all be made alive. But every man in his own order: Christ the first-fruits; afterward they that are Christ's at His coming.

*[Then cometh the end, when He shall have delivered up the kingdom to God, even the Father; when He shall have put down all rule, and all authority and power. For He must reign till He hath put all enemies under His feet. The last enemy that shall be destroyed is death. For He hath put all things under His feet. But when He saith, All things are put under Him, it is manifest that He is excepted which did put all things under Him. And when all things shall be subdued unto Him, then shall the Son also Himself be subject unto Him that put all things under Him, that God may be all in all. Else what shall they do which are baptized for the dead, if the dead rise not at all? why are they then baptized for the dead? And why stand we in jeopardy every hour? I protest by your rejoicing which I have in Christ Jesus our Lord, I die daily. If after the manner

* The passage within brackets may be omitted.

of men I have fought with beasts at Ephesus, what advantageth it to me if the dead rise not? let us eat and drink; for to-morrow we die. Be not deceived: evil communications corrupt good manners. Awake to righteousness, and sin not; for some have not the knowledge of God: I speak this to your shame.]

But some man will say, How are the dead raised up? and with what body do they come? Thou fool, that which thou sowest is not quickened except it die. And that which thou sowest, thou sowest not that body that shall be, but bare grain, it may chance of wheat, or of some other grain; but God giveth it a body as it hath pleased Him, and to every seed his own body. *[All flesh is not the same flesh: but there is one kind of flesh of men, another flesh of beasts, another of fishes, and another of birds. There are also celestial bodies, and bodies terrestrial: but the glory of the celestial is one, and the glory of the terrestrial is another. There is one glory of the sun, and another glory of the moon, and another glory of the stars; for one star differeth from another star in glory.] So also is the resurrection of the dead: it is sown in corruption, it is raised in incorruption: it is sown in dishonour, it is raised in glory: it is sown in weakness, it is raised in power: it is sown a natural body, it is raised a spiritual body.

* The passage within brackets may be omitted.

There is a natural body, and there is a spiritual body. And so it is written, The first Adam was made a living soul, the last Adam was made a quickening spirit. Howbeit that was not first which is spiritual, but that which is natural; and afterward that which is spiritual. The first man is of the earth, earthy; the second man is the Lord from heaven. As is the earthy, such are they also that are earthy: and as is the heavenly, such are they also that are heavenly. And as we have borne the image of the earthy, we shall also bear the image of the heavenly. Now this I say, brethren, that flesh and blood cannot inherit the kingdom of God; neither doth corruption inherit incorruption. Behold, I show you a mystery; we shall not all sleep, but we shall all be changed, in a moment, in the twinkling of an eye, at the last trump (for the trumpet shall sound); and the dead shall be raised incorruptible, and we shall be changed. For this corruptible must put on incorruption, and this mortal must put on immortality. So when this corruptible shall have put on incorruption, and this mortal shall have put on immortality, then shall be brought to pass the saying that is written, Death is swallowed up in victory. O death, where is thy sting? O grave, where is thy victory? The sting of death is sin; and the strength of sin is the law. But thanks be to God, which giveth us the victory through our Lord Jesus Christ. Therefore, my beloved brethren, be ye steadfast, unmovable, always abounding in the work of the Lord, forasmuch as ye know that your labour is not in vain in the Lord.

2 *Corinthians* iv. 17, 18, v. 1-10.

Our light affliction, which is but for a moment, worketh for us a far more exceeding and eternal weight of glory; while we look not at the things which are seen, but at the things which are not seen: for the things which are seen are temporal, but the things which are not seen are eternal. For we know that if our earthly house of this tabernacle were dissolved, we have a building of God, an house not made with hands, eternal in the heavens. For in this we groan, earnestly desiring to be clothed upon with our house which is from heaven: if so be that being clothed we shall not be found naked. For we that are in this tabernacle do groan, being burdened; not for that we would be unclothed, but clothed upon, that mortality might be swallowed up of life. Now He that hath wrought us for the self-same thing is God, who also hath given unto us the earnest of the Spirit. Therefore we are always confident, knowing that, whilst we are at home in the body, we are absent from the Lord (for we walk by faith, not by sight): we are confident, I say, and willing rather to be absent from the body, and to be present with the Lord. Wherefore we labour, that whether present or absent, we may be accepted of Him. For we must all appear before the judgment-seat of Christ; that every one may receive the things done in his body, according to that he hath done, whether it be good or bad.

1 *Thessalonians* iv. 13-18.

I would not have you to be ignorant, brethren, concerning them which are asleep, that ye sorrow not, even as others which have no hope. For if we believe that Jesus died and rose again, even so them also which sleep in Jesus will God bring with Him. For this we say unto you by the word of the Lord, that we which are alive and remain unto the coming of the Lord, shall not prevent them which are asleep. For the Lord himself shall descend from heaven with a shout, with the voice of the archangel, and with the trump of God; and the dead in Christ shall rise first: then we which are alive and remain shall be caught up together with them in the clouds, to meet the Lord in the air: and so shall we ever be with the Lord. Wherefore comfort one another with these words.

2 Peter iii. 10-14.

The day of the Lord will come as a thief in the night; in the which the heavens shall pass away with a great noise, and the elements shall melt with fervent heat, the earth also and the works that are therein shall be burnt up. Seeing then that all these things shall be dissolved, what manner of persons ought ye to be in all holy conversation and godliness, looking for and hasting unto the coming of the day of God, wherein the heavens being on fire shall be dissolved, and the elements shall melt with fervent heat? Nevertheless we, according to His promise, look for new heavens and a new earth, wherein dwelleth righteousness. Wherefore, beloved, seeing that ye look for such things, be diligent that ye may be found of Him in peace, without spot, and blameless.

Revelation vii. 9-17.

After this I beheld, and, lo, a great multitude, which no man could number, of all nations, and kindreds, and people, and tongues, stood before the throne, and before the Lamb, clothed with white robes, and palms in their hands; and cried with a loud voice, saying, Salvation to our God which sitteth upon the throne, and unto the Lamb. And all the angels stood round about the throne, and about the elders and the four beasts, and fell before the throne on their faces and worshipped God, saying, Amen : Blessing, and glory, and wisdom, and thanksgiving, and honour, and power, and might, be unto our God for ever and ever. Amen. And one of the elders answered, saying unto me, What are these which are arrayed in white robes ? and whence came they ? And I said unto him, Sir, thou knowest. And he said to me, These are they which came out of great tribulation, and have washed their robes, and made them white in the blood of the Lamb. Therefore are they before the throne of God, and serve Him day and night in His temple : and He that sitteth on the throne shall dwell among them. They shall hunger no more, neither thirst any more, neither shall the sun light on them, nor any heat. For the Lamb, which is in the midst of the throne, shall feed them, and shall lead them unto living fountains of waters ; and God shall wipe away all tears from their eyes.

Revelation xx. 11-13.

And I saw a great white throne, and Him that sat on it, from whose face the earth and the heaven fled away ; and there was found no place for them. And I saw the dead, small and

great, stand before God : and the books were
opened ; and another book was opened, which
is the book of life : and the dead were judged
out of those things which were written in the
books, according to their works. And the sea
gave up the dead which were in it ; and death
and hell delivered up the dead which were
in them ; and they were judged every man according to their works.

Revelation xxi. 1-7.

And I saw a new heaven and a new earth:
for the first heaven and the first earth were passed
away ; and there was no more sea. And I John
saw the holy city, new Jerusalem, coming down
from God out of heaven, prepared as a bride
adorned for her husband. And I heard a great
voice out of heaven, saying, Behold, the tabernacle of God is with men, and He will dwell
with them, and they shall be His people, and
God himself shall be with them, and be their
God. And God shall wipe away all tears from
their eyes ; and there shall be no more death,
neither sorrow nor crying, neither shall there be
any more pain : for the former things are passed
away. And He that sat upon the throne said,
Behold, I make all things new. And He said
unto me, Write : for these words are true and
faithful. And He said unto me, It is done.

I am Alpha and Omega, the beginning and the end: I will give unto him that is athirst of the fountain of the water of life freely. He that overcometh shall inherit all things; and I will be his God, and he shall be my son.

Thereafter may be used such portions of the service following, and at such time, as shall be convenient, in the discretion of the Minister:

Man that is born of a woman hath but a short time to live, and is full of misery. He cometh up, and is cut down, like a flower; he fleeth as it were a shadow, and never continueth in one stay.

In the midst of life we are in death: of whom may we seek for succour, but of Thee, O Lord, who for our sins art justly displeased?

Yet, O Lord God most holy, O Lord most mighty, O holy and most merciful Saviour, deliver us not into the bitter pains of eternal death.

Thou knowest, Lord, the secrets of our hearts: shut not thy merciful ears to our prayer, but spare us, Lord most holy, O God most mighty; O holy and merciful Saviour, Thou most worthy Judge eternal, suffer us not at our last hour, for any pains of death, to fall from Thee.

Forasmuch as it hath pleased Almighty God, in His wise Providence, to take out of this world the soul of our deceased *brother*, we therefore commit *his* body to the ground ; earth to earth, ashes to ashes, dust to dust; looking for the general resurrection in the last day, and the life of the world to come, through our Lord Jesus Christ; at whose second coming in glorious majesty, to judge the world, the earth and sea shall give up their dead ; and the corruptible bodies of those who sleep in Him shall be changed, and made like unto His own glorious body, according to the mighty working whereby He is able to subdue all things unto Himself.*

Or this:

The dust returns to dust, and the spirit to God who gave it : therefore do we now commit the body of our departed *brother* to the earth [*or* deep] until that hour when earth and sea shall give up their dead, at the coming of our Lord Jesus Christ to judge the world.

I heard a voice from heaven, saying unto me, Write, From henceforth blessed are the dead which die in the Lord : even so, saith the Spirit, for they rest from their labours.—Rev. xiv. 13.

Blessed be the God and Father of our Lord Jesus Christ, which according to His abundant

---

* *At the burial of the dead at sea, instead of the words*, We therefore commit *his* body to the ground, earth to earth, &c., *shall be said*, We therefore commit *his* body to the deep, to be turned into corruption, looking for the general resurrection, &c.

mercy hath begotten us again unto a lively hope by the resurrection of Jesus Christ from the dead, to an inheritance incorruptible, and undefiled, and that fadeth not away.—1 Pet. i. 3, 4.

Let us Pray.

OUR Father which art in heaven, Hallowed be Thy name. Thy kingdom come. Thy will be done in earth, as it is in heaven. Give us this day our daily bread. And forgive us our trespasses as we forgive them that trespass against us. And lead us not into temptation, but deliver us from evil.
Amen.

ALMIGHTY God, with whom do live the spirits of them that depart hence in the Lord, and with whom the souls of the faithful, after they are delivered from the burden of the flesh, are in joy and felicity; We give Thee hearty thanks that it pleaseth Thee to deliver them out of the miseries of this sinful world; beseeching Thee, of Thy gracious goodness, shortly to accomplish the number of Thine elect, and to hasten Thy kingdom; that we, with all those that are departed in the true faith of Thy holy name, may have our perfect consummation and bliss, both in body and soul, in Thy eternal and everlasting glory; through Jesus Christ our Lord.

Amen.

O MERCIFUL God, the Father of our Lord Jesus Christ, who is the resurrection and the life; in whom whosoever believeth shall live, though he die; and whosoever liveth and believeth in Him shall not die eternally; who also hath taught us by His holy apostle S. Paul, not to be sorry, as men without hope, for them that sleep in Him; We meekly beseech Thee, O Father, to raise us from the death of sin unto the life of righteousness; that, when we shall depart this life, we may rest in Him; and that, at the general resurrection in the last day, we may be found acceptable in Thy sight, and receive that blessing which Thy well-beloved Son shall then pronounce to all that love and fear Thee, saying, Come, ye blessed children of my Father, receive the kingdom prepared for you from the beginning of the world: grant this, we beseech Thee, O merciful Father, through Jesus Christ, our Mediator and Redeemer.

Amen.

O GOD, whose days are without end, and whose mercies cannot be numbered; Make us, we beseech Thee, deeply sensible of the shortness and uncertainty of human life, and

let Thy Holy Spirit lead us through this vale of misery, in holiness and righteousness, all the days of our lives: that, when we shall have served Thee in our generation, we may be gathered unto our fathers, having the testimony of a good conscience; in the communion of the catholic Church; in the confidence of a certain faith; in the comfort of a reasonable, religious, and holy hope; in favour with Thee our God, and in perfect charity with the world: all which we ask through Jesus Christ our Lord.
Amen.

NOW the God of peace, that brought again from the dead our Lord Jesus Christ, that great Shepherd of the sheep, through the blood of the everlasting covenant, make you perfect in every good work to do His will, working in you that which is well-pleasing in His sight, through Jesus Christ; to whom be glory for ever and ever.
Amen.

THE grace of the Lord Jesus Christ, and the love of God, and the fellowship of the Holy Ghost, be with you all evermore.
Amen.

Ordination Service.

ORDINATION OF MINISTERS.

THE Reformed Church, in all its branches, even those which, through the force of circumstances or from choice, retained a form of government more or less prelatical, was united in holding that there is no *order* (in the theological sense of the term) of the Christian Ministry, essentially and *jure divino*, superior to that of Presbyter, or Minister of the Word and Sacraments. It did not assert that any precise Constitution is laid down in Scripture, in accordance with which the Presbyters of Churches are to exercise uniformly at all times and in all lands their governmental functions; nor did it deny the lawfulness or, in certain circumstances, the expediency of such National Church Constitutions as may, with the consent of the whole body, have committed to some Presbyters the exercise of higher functions and greater power than others. But it maintained that all such Constitutions are matters of human arrangement, and subject to the control of the Church, which, when required by the paramount interests of truth and righteousness, can modify or annul the special jurisdiction it has bestowed.

Among the many proofs of this, it is sufficient to quote two passages—the one from Calvin, styled by some the Father of Presbytery, and the other from Hooker, the great defender of the Episcopal Constitution of the Church of England. "Show us," says the former, "a hierarchy in which the Bishops are distinguished, but not for their refusing to be subject to Christ; in which they depend upon Him as their only head, and act solely with reference to Him; in which they cultivate brotherly fellowship with each other, bound together with no other tie than His truth; then, indeed, I will confess that there is no anathema too strong for those who do not regard such Bishops with reverence, and yield them the fullest obedience." *

* Tractat. de Reformandà Ecclesiâ.

"Therefore," writes Hooker, "they [Bishops] must acknowledge that the Church hath power, by universal consent, upon urgent cause, to take it [their power] away, if thereunto she be constrained through the proud, tyrannical, and unreformable dealings of her Bishops, whose regiment she hath thus long delighted in because she hath found it good and requisite to be so governed. Wherefore, lest Bishops forget themselves, as if none on earth had authority to touch their states, let them continually bear in mind that it is rather the force of custom, whereby the Church, having so long found it good to continue under the regiment of her virtuous Bishops, doth still uphold, maintain, and honour them in that respect, than that any true and heavenly law can be showed, by the evidence whereof it may of a truth appear that the Lord Himself hath appointed Presbyters for ever to be under the regiment of Bishops, in what sort soever they behave themselves. Let this consideration be a bridle unto them; let it teach them not to disdain the advice of their Presbyters, but to use their authority with so much the greater humility and moderation, as a sword which the Church hath power to take from them."*

* Ecclesiastical Polity, vii. 5.

ORDINATION SERVICE. 297

The extreme dogmas of those who maintained, on the one hand, that Episcopacy is essential, and, on the other, that it is unlawful, were matters of after-thought, the result of unhappy circumstances, and are both alike heretical deviations from the large and catholic tenet of the Reformers.

As a consequence of the persuasion that there is no order of the Ministry essentially, or by divine right, superior to that of Presbyter, the Reformed Church, while holding, in accordance with Scripture and sound sense, that the Ministry is to be maintained through the trial and ordination thereto of men in perpetual succession by those who have themselves been invested therewith, denies that for the functions of trial and ordination any such distinct and superior order is required. It maintains that those who have been intrusted with authority to discharge the other high and holy duties of the Ministry are competent, when acting in an orderly collegiate capacity—that is, as the Presbytery of a Church—to admit others to the same status ; and although, by the constitution or custom of various branches of the Church, special power and more prominent functions in trial and ordination have been assigned to certain Ministers, under the titles of Bishop, Superintendent, Præpositus, Moderator, President, &c., with greater or less dignity and permanence, it asserts that, in all such cases, ordination is valid, as being the act not merely of the officiating dignitary, but of the Presbyterate of the Church, of whom he is the acknowledged representative, with whose concurrence, expressed or implied, he lays on his hands, and through whom the stream of succession, in the sense in which that term is understood by Protestants, flows.

On the other hand, the Scriptures, while setting forth no *order* superior to Presbyters—even Apostles being included under that name [*]—plainly mentions a difference in the *offices* or *functions* of the Ministry, founded upon the different qualifications or gifts bestowed on individuals, and the spheres in which, according to the various requirements of the Church, these qualifications are to be exercised, "for the perfecting of the saints, for the work of the Ministry, for the edifying of the body of Christ." Of such offices we have an express enumeration in Eph. iv. 11 — Apostles, Prophets, Evangelists, Pastors, Teachers. Of these it was uniformly held by the Reformed divines that the two for-

[*] 1 Peter, v. i.

mer offices—those of Apostle and Prophet—were extraordinary and temporary, ceasing with the special qualifications on which they were founded, and that the two latter are ordinary and perpetual. As regards the office of Evangelist, it must, it is feared, be admitted that the very inadequate sense of missionary obligation in the Reformed Churches—caused, if not justified, by the absorption of their energies in defending their own position—led to its being frequently classified with the temporary and extraordinary offices. But certainly, as the gifts necessary for the work of Evangelization have not ceased, so neither can the necessity for the office cease until the whole world has been Evangelized; and the revived sense of missionary obligation has gradually led to the general recognition, throughout the branches of the Reformed Church, of the office of Evangelist or Missionary, along with those of Pastor (or Bishop in the New Testament sense) and of Teacher or Doctor, as permanent.

The necessity of such a threefold Ministry as this, and the adaptation of its separate functions alike to the nature of man, as a being compounded of intellect, emotion, and will or activity —all of which it is the object of religion to influence and to sanctify—and to the obvious wants of the Church and the world, it would be out of place here to discuss at length. It is true that more than one of these functions may, nay, often must, be exercised by the same individual. Thus, the Evangelist must be, to a certain extent, a Teacher—that is, must found his appeals to the heart or emotional nature upon divine truths clearly presented to the intellect. The Teacher, or Doctor, in order to the right and profitable discharge of his special function, must imbue his reasonings with an evangelic spirit and unction. And the Pastor must be a Teacher as regards the ignorance, and an Evangelist as regards the carelessness and hard-heartedness of his flock, as well as the spiritual Guide and moral Ruler [Bishop] of their lives. Still, it is not the less evident that each of these functions has its special characteristic and object, and that any branch of the Church has but an incomplete view of its position, and is inadequately fitted for its whole duty—"the perfecting of the saints, the work of the ministry, and the edifying of the body of Christ"—which does not recognise and provide for the exercise of all these distinct offices; which does not give an express place and due honour, in its system and in the ranks of its Ministry, to the special gifts and functions of the Evangelist and of the Teacher, as well as to the ordinary and general office of the Pastor.

It must, however, be admitted that, in the Church of Scotland, the *pastoral* office having long been the only one of the three to any extent practically exemplified, Ordination to the Ministry of the Word and Sacraments, although always viewed by her as an act investing the person ordained with the character of a Presbyter of the Church Catholic or Universal,* came to be so exclusively connected with institution to the office of Pastor in a special charge, as to lead to much confusion of ideas in the popular mind. For the instances of persons being ordained with a view to the functions of Teacher in the Seminaries of the Church were, owing to the fact that those nominated to Theological Professorships had, in almost every case, been previously parochial Pastors, too rare to keep before the public the distinction between Order and Office—between the Presbyterate or general character and status of Minister, and the various accidents of a particular function or

* See Jus Divinum Ministerii Evangelici ; Hill, VI. ii. 2, and others.

charge; while the Ordination of a person without a fixed pastoral cure, with a view to the most difficult and honourable function of the Gospel Ministry, that of a Missionary or Evangelist, was spoken of somewhat slightingly as Ordination to a *ministerium vagum*. This is but one among several instances in which the Scottish Church, while cherishing the persuasion of its being the most exact exemplification of the principles and polity of the Reformed Church, has lapsed into a sort of insular provincialism. For it is scarcely necessary to say that in the Reformed Churches of Switzerland, and most other countries of Europe, the two ideas, of Order on the one hand, and Function on the other, have been preserved from the first, and that Ordination to the Ministry and Institution to Office are kept entirely distinct, a separate ceremonial being provided for each.

In the following services an attempt has been made, as far as custom seems at present to admit, to preserve this distinction, as well as that between the three great functions of the Ministry. Some portions of the prayers will recall the formularies of the Reformed Churches to those who have studied them.

In most of the Reformed Churches, the Act of Ordination and imposition of hands, instead of being included, as with us, in the Ordination prayer, either precedes or follows it, the formula being addressed to the Candidate. There appears to be no good reason for preferring the one mode to the other.

It is worthy of being considered by Scottish Presbyteries whether it might not be advantageous, on the occasion of Ordinations and Inductions, more generally to commit the conduct of the Service, as is done in some Churches, to more members of the Presbytery than one ; assigning the Presidency, with the Act of Ordination and the Charge to the Minister, to some member whose years and experience mark him out as most suitable for such functions, the Sermon and other offices being allotted to others. Certainly the custom of intrusting the whole of the Services on occasions of such solemnity to the youngest member of the body, has little to recommend it, and especially as respects the Ordaining Prayer and the Charge, is very generally felt to be at variance with natural propriety and edification.

ORDINATION SERVICE.

Divine Service shall be celebrated according to the usual order, or to such special order as the Presbytery may judge proper, by one or more Ministers appointed for the purpose.*

After the Sermon, the presiding Minister shall read from the pulpit a Narrative, previously approved by the Presbytery, of the proceedings of the Presbytery preparatory to the solemnity in hand, concluding with these words:

All having accordingly been so far done in this matter as is required by the law and usage of the Church, the Presbytery will now proceed † to ordain the said A. B. to the Holy Ministry [and thereafter to receive and admit him to the office of   ] as soon as he shall have

---

* See Table of Scripture Lessons and Psalms, &c., at the end.

† When a Minister already ordained is merely to be inducted into a new office, the words will be as follows:—" The Presbytery will now proceed to receive and admit the said A. B. to the office of   , as soon," &c.

ORDINATION SERVICE. 305

answered satisfactorily the questions appointed by the Church.

Then the Candidate, standing up in the face of the Congregation present, shall answer the questions appointed by the Church to be put to those who are to be ordained to the Ministry or admitted to any charge.

These questions, according to Act 10, *Assembly* 1711,* *are as follows :*

1. Do you believe the Scriptures of the Old and New Testaments to be the Word of God, and the only rule of faith and manners? *Answer*—I do.

2. Do you sincerely own and believe the whole doctrine contained in the Confession of Faith, approven by the General Assemblies of this Church, and ratified by law in the year 1690, to be founded upon the Word of God;

---

* In the Act "for settling the quiet and peace of the Church"—1st William and Mary (1693) cap. 22—it is ordained " That no person be admitted a minister or preacher within the bounds of this Church unless that he . . . subscribes the Confession of Faith, declaring the same to be the confession of his faith, and that he owns the doctrine therein contained to be the true doctrine, which he will constantly adhere to ; as likewise that he owns and acknowledges Presbyterian Church government . . . to be the only government of this Church, and that he will submit thereto and concur therewith, and never endeavour, directly or indirectly, the prejudice or subversion thereof."

The Church, by its own Act, Act of Assembly X., 1711, imposed the existing more minute and stringent formula.

U

and do you acknowledge the same as the confession of your faith; and will you firmly and constantly adhere thereto, and to the utmost of your power assert, maintain, and defend the same, and the purity of worship as presently practised in this national Church, and asserted in Act 15, Assembly 1707, entitled, Act against innovations in the worship of God? *Answer*—I so believe and promise.

3. Do you disown all Popish, Arian, Socinian, Arminian, Bourignian, and other doctrines, tenets, and opinions whatsoever contrary to or inconsistent with the foresaid Confession of Faith? *Answer*—I do.

4. Are you persuaded that the Presbyterian government and discipline of this Church are founded upon the Word of God, and agreeable thereto, and do you promise to submit to the said government and discipline, and to concur with the same, and never to endeavour, directly or indirectly, the prejudice or subversion thereof, but to the utmost of your power, in your station, to maintain, support, and defend the said discipline and Presbyterian government by kirk-sessions, presbyteries, provincial synods, and General Assemblies, during all the days of your life? *Answer*—I so believe and promise.

5. Do you promise to submit yourself willingly and humbly, in the spirit of meekness, unto the admonitions of the brethren of this

Presbytery, and to be subject to them and all other Presbyteries, and superior judicatories of this Church, where God in His providence shall cast your lot: and that according to your power you shall maintain the unity and peace of this Church against error and schism, notwithstanding of whatever trouble or persecution may arise, and that you shall follow no divisive course from the present established doctrine, worship, discipline, and government of this Church? *Answer*—I do.

6. Are not zeal for the honour of God, love to Jesus Christ, and desire of saving souls your great motives and chief inducements to enter into the function of the holy ministry, and not worldly designs and interest? Answer—I trust so.

7. Have you used any undue methods, either by yourself or others, in procuring this call? *Answer*—I have not.

8. Do you engage, in the strength and grace of Jesus Christ our Lord and Master, to rule well your own family, to live a holy and circumspect life, and faithfully, diligently, and cheerfully to discharge all the parts of the ministerial work, to the edification of the body of Christ? *Answer*—I do, trusting to the help of God.

[9. Do you accept of, and close with, the call to be pastor of this parish, and promise through

grace to perform all the duties of a faithful minister of the gospel among this people? *
Answer—I do, trusting to the help of God.]

Then may be sung Psalm lxviii. 18-20.

    Thou hast, O Lord, most glorious,
      ascended up on high;
    And in triumph victorious led
      captive captivity;
    Thou hast received gifts for men,
      for such as did rebel;
    Yea, ev'n for them, that God the Lord
      in midst of them might dwell.

    Bless'd be the Lord, who is to us
      of our salvation God;
    Who daily with His benefits
      us plenteously doth load.
    He of salvation is the God,
      who is our God most strong;
    And unto God the Lord from death
      the issues do belong.

The presiding Presbyter shall then descend from the pulpit, and shall pray as follows, the person to be ordained kneeling before him, and the other Presbyters standing around:

ALMIGHTY God, eternal Fountain of light and life, we, Thine unworthy

---

* This question is to be put only when the person ordained is also to be invested with the office of pastor over the congregation present.

servants whom Thou hast called to minister unto Thee, humbly draw near to Thee, through Jesus Christ Thy well-beloved Son, our Divine Prophet, Priest, and King, whom in Thine infinite love and wisdom Thou hast given to be the Redeemer of the world, and Head over all things to Thy Church. Vouchsafe to us, O God, for His sake, Thy presence and Thy grace. O be merciful unto us, and bless us, and cause Thy face to shine upon us; that Thy way may be known upon earth; Thy saving health among all nations.

Accept, O God, the sacrifice of thanks and praise which we offer unto Thee. For all Thy love manifested in the great redemption; for all that Christ our Saviour did, and taught, and suffered; for His victory over sin and death; for His triumphant resurrection and ascension; for the gift and indwelling of the Holy Ghost; the comfort of Thy Word and ordinances; the preservation of Thy Church on earth, and the glory prepared for it in heaven; we desire, with angels and just men made perfect, and with Thy whole Church militant upon earth, to magnify and adore Thy name. Glory to God in the highest, and on earth peace, good will toward men.

Especially do we, at this time, bless Thee, that when Jesus Christ Thy Son ascended up on high, He condescended to call the children of men to be His ministers, and gave gifts unto them, that they might, as apostles and prophets, lay the foundations of His Church, and as evangelists, pastors, and teachers, in perpetual succession, enlarge and feed and guide the same, promising to be with them always, until His second coming in majesty to judge the world.

And now, O God, look down, we earnestly beseech Thee, with favour upon this Thy servant, who is called and offers himself to take part in this great work. Cleanse him from all iniquity; purify and comfort his heart. And as we, in Thy name, do* by the imposition of our hands, ordain him a Presbyter in Thy Church, and commit unto him authority to minister Thy Word and sacraments, O do Thou, who healest what is infirm, and suppliest what is wanting, receive and strengthen him for Thy service, giving him the unction of the Holy Ghost.

Increase in him all needful gifts of Thy grace. Give him a true understanding and a firm belief of Thy holy Word, that knowing himself the power thereof, he may faithfully and effectually make it known to others. Endue him with a burning zeal for Thy glory and for the salvation of men. Sanctify him in body, soul, and spirit.

---

* Here the presiding Presbyter shall lay his hands upon the head of the candidate, the other Presbyters standing near laying on each his right hand.

Guide, uphold, and prosper him in all the work of his ministry, to the praise of Thy name, the advancement of Thy kingdom, the comfort of Thy Church, and the discharge of his own conscience in the day of the Lord Jesus, to whom, with Thee, O Father, and the Holy Spirit, be all honour and glory, world without end.

        Amen.

The person ordained then standing up, the presiding Presbyter, and the others in succession, shall take him by the right hand, saying:

We give you the right hand of fellowship, to take part with us in this ministry.

The presiding Presbyter shall then return to the pulpit, and if the person ordained is, at the same time, to be instituted by Act of the Presbytery to the office of Pastor of a Church, or any other office, shall add these words:

In the name of the Lord Jesus Christ, and by appointment of this Presbytery, I receive and admit you to the office of . And may grace, mercy, and peace, from God the Father, Son, and Holy Ghost, be with you always.

        Amen.

Thereafter the presiding Presbyter shall give a solemn charge to the new Minister, and (if he is at the same time inducted as a Pastor) to the people present, setting forth their respective duties from the Word of God.

Then shall be offered the following Prayer, at the Institution of a Pastor:

ALMIGHTY God, who, under Thine ever-blessed Son, the Great Shepherd of Thy sheep, hast appointed them to be fed and guided by Thy ministering servants; we thank Thee that Thou hast this day graciously provided a Pastor for a portion of Thy flock; and we earnestly entreat Thee to grant unto Thy servant to whom this solemn charge is now committed by us in Thy name, Thy Holy Spirit, to fit him more and more for the work to which he has been called. Give him utterance that he may boldly make known Thy Word and will, and faithfully dispense the mysteries of Thy Gospel. Endue him with wisdom and valour to rule aright the people over whom he is set, and to preserve them in peace and purity, so that Thy Church under his administration and example may increase in numbers and in holiness. Grant him meekness, patience, and firmness to bear all the trials and troubles of his ministry, and strengthen him with Thy Spirit, that he may abide steadfast to the end, and be received, with all Thy faithful servants, into the joy of his Lord. Give grace also to those over whom he has been appointed, that they may reverently receive his doctrine and godly admonitions, yielding him all due respect and obedience according to Thy holy Word, and earnestly endeavouring so to profit by his labours, that they may grow in grace, and be made partakers of eternal life, through Jesus Christ our Saviour, to whom, with Thee, O Father, and with the Holy Ghost, be glory, as it was in the beginning, is now, and ever shall be, world without end.

Amen.

When the person ordained is appointed to the office or function of an Evangelist or Missionary, the following Prayer of Institution shall be used instead of that immediately preceding:

O MOST gracious and merciful God, who hast commanded Thy Gospel to be preached unto all nations, that the ends of the earth may see Thy Salvation; we give Thee thanks that, from age to age, Thou dost inspire Thy chosen servants with a desire to make known Thy truth to those who are sitting in darkness, that they may be delivered from sin and death, and made partakers of our hope and joy. And we beseech Thee greatly to bless Thy servant here before Thee, whom in Thy name we send forth to this good work. O strengthen his hands and encourage his heart for all the special dangers and difficulties and temptations that may lie before him. In all his trials may his faith in Thy promises and love abide unshaken, and his hope be constant in Thee. Grant him grace to preach boldly and faithfully the unsearchable riches of Christ, to instruct with meekness those who are opposed to the truth, and to gather into the sheepfold of Christ many who are wandering in the ways of error and of sin. Give him a mouth and wisdom, which all the adversaries he may encounter shall not be able to gainsay or to resist. Grant that going forth in meekness of wisdom, and labouring in entire dependence on Thee, he may reap abundant fruit of his labours in the conversion of souls unto Christ, and obtain the reward of a faithful servant in Thy heavenly kingdom, when they who have turned many unto righteousness shall shine as the stars for ever. These blessings, and all that Thou seest to be for the good of Thy servant and the honour of Thy name, we earnestly implore, through Jesus Christ Thy Son, to whom, with the Father and the Holy Ghost, be all praise and glory, world without end.

Amen.

When the person ordained is instituted to the office or function of a Teacher or Doctor in a School of Theology, or Seminary of the Church, the Prayer of Institution shall be as follows:—

O GOD, our heavenly Father, who, when we were sunk in darkness and sin, didst send Thy Son to be the Light of the World, and whose Word and Spirit alone can guide us into the way of truth and happiness; send down, we pray Thee, Thy blessing on this Thy servant, now appointed to discharge the office of a teacher in Thy Church, and to make known the mysteries of Thy Holy Gospel. Strengthen all his faculties, inspire him with a pure and fervent love of the truth, as it is in Jesus, and grant that by earnest study and prayer he may daily grow in the understanding of Thy Word, and become mighty in the knowledge of the Scripture. Give him wisdom, faithfulness, and skill to teach Thy truth, and to uphold it against all false doctrine. And graciously preserve those who shall be committed to his care from all error and delusion, that they be not spoiled through philosophy and vain deceit, after the tradition of men and the rudiments of the world; but grant that their faith standing not in the wisdom of men, but in the power of God, they may be fitted both to defend and to extend in this dark world the saving knowledge of Jesus Christ Thy Son, in whom are hid all the treasures of knowledge and wisdom, and to whom, with Thee the Father and the Holy Spirit, we ascribe all honour and glory, now and for ever.

     Amen.

The Service shall conclude with singing, and the following Benediction:

NOW the God of Peace, that brought again from the dead our Lord Jesus Christ, that great Shepherd of the Sheep, through the blood of the everlasting covenant, make you perfect in every good work to do His will, working in you that which is well pleasing in His sight, through Jesus Christ, to whom be glory, for ever and ever.

 Amen.

  NOTE.—*That where a person previously ordained is inducted to a pastoral or other office, the presiding Minister shall, immediately after receiving satisfactory answers to the questions prescribed by the Church, pass on to the words:* In the name of the Lord Jesus Christ, and by appointment of this Presbytery, I receive and admit you to the office, &c. *And shall then proceed to the Charge and Prayer of Institution.*

ORDINATION SERVICE.

Lessons of Scripture proper for the Service preceding the Ordination of Ministers, and their Induction to office.

I.

Isaiah, vi. 1-8.
xxxv.
xl. 1-11.
xlix.

Isaiah, lii. 7—end.
lxi.
lxii.
Ezekiel, xxxiii. 1-9.

II.

Matt. xxviii.
Luke, x. 1-24.
John, x. 1-16.
Acts, xx. 17-38.
1 Cor. ii.
iii.

1 Cor. iv.
Eph. iv. 1-16.
1 Tim. iii. 1-7.
2 Tim. ii.
iii. & iv. to v. 8.
1 Peter, v.

Portions of Psalms, &c., proper to be sung.

Psalm lxxviii. 4-7, "The praises of the Lord our God," &c.; lxxxix. 15-18; xcvi. 1-6; xcviii. 1-4. Paraph. xviii. 1-4; xx. 1-4; xxiii. 1-5 and 7-10.

At the end of the Service.

Psalm xxiii., lxvii., lxxii. 17—end; lxxx. 14, 15, 18, 19; lxxxix. 25—end; cxvii., cxxi., cxxxii. 13—end. Paraph. xix. 4—end; xxiii. 12—end; liv.

THE END.

www.ingramcontent.com/pod-product-compliance
Lightning Source LLC
Chambersburg PA
CBHW030735230426
43667CB00007B/721